DERISION POINTS

Clown Prince Bush the W

(the Real Story of his "Decision Points")

ProgRESSive

2010

DERISION POINTS
Clown Prince Bush the W:
the Real Story of his
"Decision Points"

Cover photo: "President Bush's Technology Agenda," from http://georgewbush-whitehouse.archives.gov. Clown on back cover: WizardofWhimsy.

Published by Progressive Press,
PO Box 126, Joshua Tree, Calif. 92252,
www.ProgressivePress.com
New edition, November 2010

Length: 70,000 words, 190 pages.
Reading Ease: Flesch Kincaid Grade Level 3.0

ISBN 1-61577-243-X
EAN 978-1-61577-243-8
LCCN: 2010513600

Topics:
Juvenile career of Geo. W. "Dubya" Bush,
his rowdy behavior and drinking habits,
and assisted rise to high office.
The Power of the Swill.
Hijinks at Yale and Harvard.
Inside the Bush Family.

BISAC Subject Area Codes:
BIO011000 Biography, Heads of State
HUM006000 Humor, Political
JUV039040 Juvenile Fiction - Alcohol Abuse

The Imaginative Memoir of George W. Bush's

Unlikely Rise to Power*

*To You, The Reader:

The author was a witness to, and participant in, some of the real or imagined scenes in this book. He calls the work fact-based fiction. You may recognize many of the players and locations. The story line is authentic in some cases. It contains mostly created dialogue.

Chapters

Chapter I
Mommy Nearest

"George, will you give that kid a smack?" a hysterical Barbara Bush yelled to her husband. He was tying flies in his Kennebunkport shed. "I can't take his whining and screaming anymore," she cried.

Welcome to life with the Bushies. This was circa 1946. Barbara is a lonely, harried, dutiful housewife. She has a 4-month-old baby. It's her first. Her husband's biggest problem is trying to figure out how to catch more fish. He'd fish near their Maine summer compound.

She begged for kids. Now it was her problem.

It was George W. Bush.

George Walker Bush was the first kid born to blue-blood Brahmin George Herbert Walker Bush and Barbara Pierce Bush. He came into the world on July 6, 1946. George W. Bush greeted his son in to the world. He then quickly sprinted out the front door of the ivy-covered brick New Haven (Connecticut) Medical Center. The hospital had a wing named for his family. He was late - for a golf date. It was midsummer. It was great golfing weather. Preppy Poppy was what his parents had called him. He didn't want to miss out on a golf game. He didn't want to miss a few cocktails in the clubhouse. He had a new baby boy. It was his first child. But George Herbert Walker Bush also had another priority. It was improving his golf game. He drove over to Yale Country Club. He parked his 1944 Lincoln in the gravel, tree-lined lot. He headed for the pro shop. There, he kept one of his sets of clubs. The staff at YCC kept members' clubs for them. They cleaned them after each game. In Bush's case, it was simply an extension of his spoiled childhood. In the younger years, it was his mother who cleaned up after him.

"Hi Mr. Bush," said Billy Plouffe. Plouffe ran the club room in the back of the pro shop. "What's new?"

"I'm a father," Bush replied gleefully. But he sounded dismissive. "Is my tee time still good? 1 o'clock?"

"Yeah, you're all set," Plouffe replied. "I'll have your clubs waiting for you. They'll be on the first tee. Congratulations on your baby. That's pretty cool. What's his name? Or is it a girl?"

"Nope, it's a boy alright!" Dad Bush shot back. "George. George Walker Bush. 7 pounds, 9 ounces. A chip off the old block."

"Wow!" Plouffe said. "That's so cool. How is Mrs. Bush doing?"

"OK," Bush said. "She'll get through it one way or another. Hey, Billy, I'll talk to you later." Bush scampered into the white clapboard 1890 clubhouse. He made his way to the locker room. He changed into his golf spikes. He also shed his street clothes. He put on a pair of green Bobby Jones golfing slacks. He put on a white Izod knit golf shirt. The tall Bush looked the part. All Greenwich, all the time.

Bush played the first nine holes with a local stockbroker, Bill Spencer. Spencer was a millionaire. He was like everyone else at the Yale Country Club. He just loved hobnobbing with the upper crust. Spencer and Bush headed for the tenth tee. Plouffe ran out to meet them at the turn. "Hey, Mr. Bush," he shouted. "The hospital called. Your wife is ready to be picked up to go home with your new baby!"

"Oh?" Bush replied. "Hmmm. OK. Say, Billy, can you ring them back? Let them know I've got 9 more holes to play? I'll be up after that."

"OK, will do," Plouffe replied.

Nothing like a kid and a wife to get in the way of a good golf day. At least that's how Poppy saw the whole thing.

When Georgie was born, his father was just a youngster himself. No matter he had been to war. He had even gotten shot down. Debate still rages over whether Bush, the youngest-ever Navy pilot, did enough to try to save the plane. He insists he tried to save the plane. He said he bailed out as a last resort. His fellow crewmen all died in the crash at sea. But Bush was rescued by an aircraft carrier. Bush was a student at Yale. That's when his first child was born. He was captain of the Yale baseball team. He wrote in his book, "All the Best." He said he had little time for anything else. When a new baby came along, Dad Bush had no time for his name-sake.

The couple got home with their new baby. It was all over but the shouting. His father was a busy college student. Mrs. Bush had all she could do to handle this new burden. It was her first child. But she was in love with George Herbert Walker Bush. She once said he was the "handsomest thing I ever saw in my life." In October 1946, 4-month-old "Georgie" came down with inflamed tonsils. His father wrote later in "All the Best, My Life in Letters," that the kid awoke one night and "vomited absolutely everything."

And he hadn't even been drinking. (Not yet, anyway. Or at least not that anyone knew about yet.)

Georgie was a handful from Day One. His mother got sick and tired of mothering this little crying brat. The kid brat was born with a silver shot glass in his mouth. The young couple would go to their Kennebunkport seaside mansion for the summer. The fun was ruined. They had a crying, puking, spoiled kid.

"Hey, Bar," the rich G.H.W. Bush said. He was talking one night to his bride. They were at the dinner table. He had had a few glasses of Chardonnay. "Wanna fool around?" He had already refused his wife's earlier pleas to change Georgie's diaper. G.H.W. Bush had told her, "I'm the son of Prescott Bush. Men don't do diapers in my family." After getting married, the Bushes knew they wanted children. Or thought they wanted children. In November 1945 Poppy's priorities were fishing and golf.

One day he'd been out looking for bluefish off Biddeford Pool, Maine. He had gotten back to the house with nothing to show for his efforts. All he had was a scorching sunburn and headache. He opened the refrigerator. He took out a Miller. One led to two. Two led to three. Dusk arrived. G.H.W. Bush had downed a six-pack. So what if he was a man on the fast track. He was the son of a U.S. senator. He had come from a spoiled, rich family. They didn't know what it meant to work for a living. He liked his booze. He liked to fish.

Bar and Poppy tried to get used to having a little crying, vomiting baby around the house. Their marriage began showing strains. Rumors began that G.H.W. Bush was having one-night stands. He was supposedly seeing women who worked down at Allison's. Allison's was a popular nightspot in Kennebunkport. Bar had a vicious temper. She was devoted to her husband. She hated sex. She gave in to keep her husband from straying. She wanted kids. Only way to do it was to hop in the sack once in a while. She'd deaden the pain, so to speak, by having a couple of drinks herself. Usually it was a gin and tonic.

Bar also came from money. Her father had been president and chairman of the board of McCall's Publishing. She was as spoiled as her old man. As a young woman, Barbara was beautiful. She always showed a good face in public. She was tormented by an upbringing in the hands of domineering, rich parents. She was never good enough for them. The man she married was never good enough for his rich, autocratic mother and cold, insensitive father, either.

"George, you need to take Georgie to the doctor," Barbara said one summer morning. The kid was entering the "terrible 2s." The kid was sick with a fever. He ran a temperature. He was vomiting.

"Can't you take him?" Poppy yelled from the shed. "I'm getting ready to go out with Boilard for some stripers." Bob Boilard was a World War II veteran. He was a blue-collar shipyard worker. He taught Poppy to fish. The two were inseparable fishermen buddies. Barbara made three a crowd.

"Jesus, Lord," Barbara replied. "I've got some girls coming over for tea this afternoon. I need to clean the damn house. The laundry is piling up downstairs. George, will you please help me?"

"For crying out loud," her husband shot back. "Have Carol take him. I'm busy."

Barbara called the nanny, Carol Sterling, on the phone. Carol lived in Arundel. It was a blue-collar town next door. The town-meeting room often smelled like manure. "Can you come over?" Bar asked the girl. "I need you to take Georgie to the doctor in Kennebunk. He's pretty sick."

"OK," the nanny said. "Gimme a half hour." Carol drove from Arundel to Kennebunkport. The trip was like driving from the local dump to Fantasy Island. Arundel was a trashy, poor-man's town. Kennebunkport was full of spoiled, bratty rich people. They were like the Bushes. Carol drove her rusting-out 1940 Chevy. She came up the long driveway leading to the Bush's compound. The property included a beautiful shingled complex. There was a big beach house, a cottage, pool and a tennis court. The complex was ringed by the beautiful, alluring Atlantic Ocean. It was close to heaven.

Carol ended up taking the kid to the doctor in Kennebunk. Carol also revealed to the doctor, Donald Fiske, that the kid two weeks ago had somehow broken in to the liquor cabinet. He had cracked open a bottle of vodka. "He did drink some of it," she told the doctor. "His mother found him delirious on the floor. She told his father. His main concern was that the kid had ruined a good bottle of expensive vodka."

Dr. Fiske was shocked. "I never knew about this," he said to Carol. He examined the kid. "I can't believe they didn't bring him to the emergency room. They should have called me," he said.

Two days later Georgie got home from the doctor. His parents were at a cocktail party. They were at the yacht club. The kid was in Carol's care. She heard some strange noises. They were coming from the dining room. She was used to sitting in the den. She'd watch TV. She paid little attention to the little boy. She went into the dining room. She found the toddler on the floor. He had a bottle of Jim Beam.

"Gimme that," she yelled. She grabbed the bottle. She put it in a cupboard. It was over the kitchen sink. The kid began screaming. He was biting. He was fighting her.

"I want it," he kept wailing. "I want it. I want it."

He cried himself to sleep. Carol put him in bed. They would await his parents' return. They got home. The nanny broke the news.

"OK," G.H.W. Bush said. He looked down at the floor. This was his way of dealing with conflict. He tried to avoid it. His idea was, let Barbara handle this. Barbara shook her head. Tears came to her eyes. Her husband was already inebriated from the yacht-club party. He took off his blue Brooks Brothers blazer. He loosened his L.L. Bean club tie. The tie was blue with flying geese on it. He kicked off his Bass Weejuns. He poured himself some gin. He sat in front of the TV. He fell asleep on the couch. His hand was clutched around a goblet of gin.

Barbara got ready for bed. She kissed her son on the forehead. Her dream had been to have a family. It had become more like a nightmare. Her first baby was an impossible behavioral problem. "What have I done wrong?" she wondered to herself. The sound of the Atlantic was crashing against the shore just outside Georgie's bedroom window. His mother sat down on the edge of his bed. She buried her head in her hands. She cried in the darkness of his bedroom. Then she got ready for bed. She went to the master bedroom. She was alone in more ways than one.

She lay her head down on the pillow. She'd read some of Dr. Benjamin Spock's book on child-rearing. She wondered to herself. "What is going to happen? George drinks too much. Georgie is playing with liquor bottles."

Barbara tossed and turned. She couldn't sleep. At 3 a.m., her husband awoke on the den couch. The TV was on a test pattern. His gin cocktail was warm. He bent over. He grabbed his loafers. His blazer was slung over his arm. He headed for the master bedroom and walked in. He was surprised to find his wife still awake. "What the hell time is it?" he asked her.

"3 o'clock," she told him. "It's time you came to bed."

"You sound mad," he replied. She broke into sobs. "I am worried about Georgie. I don't know what the matter is with him. He's always getting into trouble. I think he needs you. He needs his father."

Her husband was too tired. He was hung-over. He didn't want to think right now about being a good father. "We'll talk tomorrow," he told his wife. He pulled the covers up to his ears.

Barbara was lying on her back. She was staring at the ceiling. She squeezed her eyes shut. She tried to stop the tears. She couldn't. Her eyes welled up with tears. Tears started dripping down her cheeks. She drew her left arm from beneath the bedspread. She wiped the tears from her face. But they just kept coming. "I'm so sad," she said to herself. The bedroom was quiet. The sound of the waves outside against the rocky shore was all that could be heard. Barbara didn't sleep at all. Her husband slept like a baby.

Motherhood was hard for Barbara. She did all the heavy lifting. Her husband was busy at school. He was either going to classes or practicing with the baseball team. The team had elected him captain. George was a popular guy on campus. He felt he was too young to have to deal with the responsibilities of fatherhood. He and his wife would drive to Kennebunkport on long weekends. During the summers they spent all the time up there.

On May 16, 1949, Barbara went to the attic in the Bush home. She fetched some suitcases. It was time to start getting ready to head up to Maine for the summer routine. She found the two brown Skyway suitcases. Her mother had given them to her when she was preparing for her honeymoon. The Skyways had nostalgic value. First, Barbara remembered that her mother had been given them by her - Barbara's - grandmother for her honeymoon with George H.W. Bush. Moreover, Barbara had used them when she and George spent their honeymoon in Bar Harbor, Maine.

They had selected Bar Harbor partly due to its name. Bar, of course, was what George called his new bride. So as they scanned the map looking for a good place to honeymoon, Barbara said, "Hey, George, I've got it! We'll go to Bar Harbor. Ya know, Bar? Hello?"

George agreed to Bar Harbor. Mostly it was because he hadn't come up with an alternative. He was just happy to keep harmony in his relationship with his stunning bride-to-be.

Bar took the suitcases down from the attic. She nearly fell as she negotiated the narrow stairs leading to it. She placed them on the bed in their master bedroom. She began filling them with underwear, polo shirts and shorts. She also made sure to put George's golf shoes in plastic bags. She also grabbed some special, small, hand towels for him to bring to the golf course. He liked to play at the Cape Arundel Country Club. The course was on the outskirts of Kennebunkport. His father and uncles had also played there. To George it was like home.

"Mummy, I hurt my finger." As Barbara looked up, Junior was standing in the doorway of her bedroom. Blood was gushing from his right hand. She rushed over to her 3-year-old son. She scooped him up and sat down on the side of the bed. She grabbed one of her husband's favorite lime-green golf towels. She began blotting the blood from her son's hand. As she examined his injury, she could see a deep gash between his middle and fourth fingers.

"What did you do?" she asked her little son. He was now screaming in pain. "Tell Mummsy what happened."

Junior was screaming so loudly it was hard to understand him when he tried to explain how he cut his hand.

"Bottle," was all his mother could decipher from her son. As she examined the wound, she found a shard of glass. She removed the glass gently with her fingers. She then took her son to the bathroom sink. She began flushing his hand with warm running water. After cleansing the gash, she wiped it dry with another of the golf towels. She wrapped it in gauze. She applied adhesive tape to keep the bandage from opening.

After bandaging Junior's hand, Barbara carried her son downstairs to try to find the broken glass. She and her son got to the bottom of the stairs. Barbara haphazardly glanced into the den. On the floor she saw a broken vodka bottle. Its contents were all over the Oriental rug that she and George had been given as a wedding present from his parents.

"Honey, what were you doing in the liquor cabinet?" Barbara asked her young son. This was not the first time that young George had gotten into a liquor cabinet. Now she was wondering whether she had removed all the glass from her son's hand wound. Barbara was also wondering the unmentionable: had her toddler son also drunk some of the bottle's contents. She looked into his eyes to see if they were bloodshot. She smelled his breath. From all appearances, her boy had drunk some of the vodka. How much, she had no idea. She called the emergency room at Compton Medical Center in Compton, Calif.

"My son broke a vodka bottle and cut his hand," she told a nurse. "I don't know what to do."

The nurse, Cheryl Delbeck, told Barbara to make sure the wound was free of glass. Delbeck also told her to watch her son over the next few minutes to see whether he seemed responsive. If Barbara were to see any changes in her boy's level of cognizance, Delbeck told her, "Bring your son in here as soon as you can."

Barbara kept her eye on her son over the next few hours. She also changed the dressing on his hand. She gave him a baby aspirin for the pain. Her packing detail was derailed by this unexpected calamity. Barbara decided to finish the suitcase work later. Now, it was nearly 5 p.m. Her husband would be home soon for dinner. Barbara went in to the kitchen to begin preparing dinner. The hour was late. She decided that tonight would be a pickup meal. It would be a little of this and a little of that. She took a cold slab of roast beef out of the refrigerator. She sliced it for sandwiches.

The side door of their house opened. "Hi honey, I'm home," George Bush yelled. "Is dinner ready? I've got to go to a meeting tonight. Business."

Barbara hid her anger. Barely had her husband arrived home than he was hurrying her to get dinner. He wanted to leave again for whatever the convenience of the reason prevailing at the moment. He walked upstairs to change his clothes. That is when he saw his favorite golf towels covered with blood. "What the hell!" he yelled down to his wife. "What in the Lord is this? My favorite towels."

Barbara bit her tongue. She tried to respond. But words escaped her. Finally her husband came down the stairs. She quietly explained what had happened. He was silent. He was mad. Why had she used his golf towels to mop up after his troublesome son?

The three Bushes sat down for a quick dinner. Georgie, as his father called him, said, "I'm not hungry." He took his right hand and swept it across the kitchen table. A glass of milk went flying across the kitchen. Half of it ended up in his father's lap. Broken glass was everywhere. Georgie started laughing. His mother was apparently in need of a good comedic release. She started laughing as she looked at her husband's shocked expression.

"Bar, why are you laughing?" her husband asked.

"Oh, George," was all she could come up with. She got up and tip-toed across the wet, glass-strewn floor. She fetched a mop.

Her husband got up and walked upstairs. He put on some dry pants. And Georgie? He sat at the table with a big grin on his face. He looked at his mother. She loved this boy so much it was hard for her to get mad at him. "Honey," she said to Georgie. "You need to be more careful."

"OK, Mummsy," he said. "Hey Mummsy, can I have some chocolate ice cream?"

"OK, honey. Just give Mommy time to clean up this milk and glass."

Her husband had by now changed into dry pants. He came downstairs. He grabbed two halves of a roast-beef sandwich from the table. "I should be home by 11," he told his wife. "See ya later, kiddo. Bye Georgie. You be good to your mother." He jumped into his Studebaker. He drove downtown. He was to meet with an oil prospector to discuss potential new sites for exploration. As a young oil tycoon, Bush was learning the ropes fast. He was also making a good salary. He was hoping that continued success would mean a growing salary. With it would eventually come stock options that would help secure him financially. Some day, he was thinking, he'd like to sit back and play golf and fish. He'd grown up in a wealthy family. He knew he needed to put in a few years of work for at least appearance's sake.

He knew his wife was bearing the brunt of bringing up young George. Her husband was away at work every day. Barbara was putting up with Georgie's antics. George senior wrote a letter to his mother that year. He described his son as having his "...mischievous and naughty spells, but I just can't picture what we would do without him." (Letter published in "All The Best," by George Bush, 1999.) He also told his mother that Barbara "... never becomes cross or irritable at (sic) him..."

For Georgie's father to raise the possibility of not having the son he had seemed strange. Did he regret marrying and starting a family at such a young age? Was he conflicted about his career plans? Thinking he wasn't living up to his mother's demanding personality? His first child was, by all accounts, a handful, even for a 3-year-old. The boy's mother was doing all she could do. Or so she thought. She was trying to raise her first child in a way that would make the rest of the family proud. She wanted to help prepare her boy for a successful life. But she often felt alone. She felt like she was in this all by herself. Her husband seemed detached, almost confused when it came to raising a child. He seemed to want to leave the child-rearing to his wife.

It was the post-war years. That didn't seem to be that unusual an approach to parenting.

"Here Honey," Barbara said. She put a bowl of chocolate ice cream on the table. It was in front of Georgie. "Now be careful. Pull your chair up, Honey."

"OK Mummsy," Georgie said. He was excited. He grabbed a spoon. He dug in to his treat. "Mummsy, can I have some milk?"

Barbara looked at her son. She was smiling. She reached down. She squeezed his head in her arms. She gave him a loving hug. This was a mischievous boy. He was also a lovable boy.

He finished his ice cream. He pushed the empty bowl to the middle of the kitchen table. "My hand hurts," he told his mother. She was putting laundry into the washing machine. The washer was in the utility room. It was off the kitchen.

"OK Honey, let Mommy get a wet washcloth." Barbara went to the linen closet. She retrieved a washcloth. She moistened it with witch hazel. She went over to her son. He was still sitting. He was at the kitchen table. "Let Mommy see your hand."

"No," he shouted, pulling away, His hand suddenly banged the empty ice-cream bowl. It went crashing to the floor. The bowl broke into dozens of pieces. Barbara sat for a moment in silence. She was unsure what to do next.

"George, you need to calm down," his mother told the boy. "Stay where you are. I'll clean up the glass."

It was always something with George Walker Bush. His parents loved him to pieces. But at the same time, they couldn't understand his seeming fits of energy. They invariably ended in disaster or some prank. His mother got up. She walked to the far corner of the kitchen. She fetched a broom. She began sweeping up the glass. Her mischievous son sat at the table. He was amusing himself. He was making believe the salt shaker was a police car. He was pretending that the salt shaker was pursuing the pepper shaker.

"Vroom, vroom, vroom!" he was saying. His mother was working to clean up his latest mess.

She finished the sweeping. Barbara reached for the dust pan. She swept up the shards of glass. She dumped it into the waste basket. It was under the kitchen sink. The phone rang. "Hello?" Barbara said. She picked up the phone.

"Hi Bar, it's Dorothy." It was Barbara's mother-in-law, Dorothy Bush. "How's things?"

"Oh, OK," Bar sighed. I was just cleaning up after Georgie. He broke an ice-cream dish. It was an accident.

"Is he OK?" Dorothy Bush asked.

"Yeah, he's fine. He's got a cut hand. It happened a few hours ago," his mother said.

"Oh? What's that from?" Dorothy asked.

"Oh, don't ask, Mom," Barbara replied. "You know Junior. It's always something."

"Yeah, isn't it, though?" the boy's grandmother laughed.

"Say, Bar, when are you all heading up to Maine?"

"The 29th, I think, Mom," Barbara said. "How about you and Dad?"

"I think we're heading up the 30th," Dorothy Bush said. "Anyway, what's Poppy up to?"

Barbara explained that her husband was out at a meeting.

"OK dear," her mother-in-law said. "I'll talk to you later."

Her husband got home. Barbara was sitting on the edge of Georgie's bed. She was reading him a book, "My Daddy the Oil Man."

"Bar, is there any roast beef left from dinner?" her husband yelled up the stairs.

"In the 'frig," she replied.

George fixed himself a roast-beef sandwich. He also made a gin and tonic.

Chapter II
Gimme That

Barbara awoke the Monday following Labor Day, 1951. It was time for young George to start school. He was five years old now. This was the day when he would begin kindergarten at Sam Houston Elementary School. His mother went to his bedroom to wake him. But he had no interest in getting out of bed. He had a squirt gun under the covers. She bent over to say, "Honey, it's time to go to school." He fired a blast from his squirt gun into her face.

"Gimme that," she fumed. "Gimme that." She grabbed for the gun, but her fingernails caught Georgie's right cheek. They inflicted a deep red scratch in his face. Blood oozed from the raw wound. The youngster started wailing. His mother wrapped her arms around her boy. She told him, "I'm sorry, Honey, but you need to go to school. You can't be squirting your mother with your squirt gun."

"Mommy," Georgie replied. "Can I have pancakes with lots of syrup?" He had a deep gash on his face. But this kid was quick to forget pain.

"Only if you get out of bed lickety-split and get ready for school," she told him

"OK, mummsy," Georgie replied.

Young George was a handful. But by now motherhood was becoming more routine for Barbara Bush. Young George was a brat. But he was always entertaining. He was at the time the Bush's only child.

Things changed soon enough. It was Dec. 20, 1949. His mother gave birth in Compton, Calif. Her new baby was named Pauline Robinson Bush. The family called her Robin. Young George, or Googen as Grandma Bush called him, now had a baby sister. That meant, of course, that he was the big brother. And oh, how he enjoyed riding herd over the small Robin.

"Gimme that," he yelled. Robin, 1 ½, tugged at his squirt gun. The gun by now was on the floor by the children's beds.

Gimme that.

They were words his mother had just shouted at him shortly after she tried to roust him from bed. Robin began screaming. Her older brother grabbed at her hand, prying it from the squirt gun. Their mother was by now in the kitchen. She was trying to make breakfast. She was hurrying. It was getting late. She had to get Georgie off to school.

She mixed up the pancake batter. George had asked for pancakes. His mother was obliging, despite his temper tantrum just minutes before. Barbara Bush quickly flashed back to her childhood. She stood motionless for a few moments. She was at the kitchen counter. Sun was streaming in the window. She thought of her mother. Her mother also used to prepare her daughter's breakfast before school. Barbara's eyes moistened. A bittersweet nostalgia overcame her. Her mother had been killed in September 1949. She was driving her husband to a train station. Barbara and her mother had been very close. Nowadays she was living in Texas. Barbara was especially lonely for her family. In Texas she knew no one. Memories of her mother brought her back east. She daydreamed about the pancakes. Her mom had made them for her.

"Mommy," Georgie yelled as he ran into the kitchen. "I want my pancakes with lots of syrup." He startled his mother. She was in a momentary trance.

"I'm making your pancakes," she said sternly. "Now go back to your room. Find your socks. You have two different socks on."

Young George threw down a pencil box. It was in his hand. He ran upstairs. He went to his bedroom. Robin was sitting on the floor. She was coloring. "Hey," George shouted to her. He leaped into the air. He landed on her head. She began wailing. Her mother rushed upstairs. She wanted to see what in the world had happened.

George was now jumping up and down. He was on his bed. He was laughing. He thought it was funny. He had jumped onto his sister's head. She sat on the floor playing quietly by herself.

"George!" his mother yelled. She cradled her little daughter. "What did you do to your sister?

"Mummsy," Georgie said. "I'm sorry. I was just playing." He then leaped into the air. He jumped from his bed. He landed on his sister's. The jump took him sailing over his mother and sister. They were now sitting on the floor together. Georgie started laughing.

"Georgie, change your socks," his mother instructed. "You can't go to school with two different socks."

Georgie jumped off the bed. He ran to the pine dresser. He quickly pulled on the sock drawer. The entire drawer was full of socks. It ended up on the floor. The corner of the drawer struck Barbara's arm. She left Robin for a moment. She grabbed her son.

"Stop," she told him. "Calm down."

Georgie changed his socks. His mother and Robin were in the kitchen. Georgie was dressed in cuffed chinos. He had on a madras plaid sport shirt. The shirt had a button-down collar. He ran into the kitchen. He plopped himself down at the Formica-and-metal breakfast table. The table had a white vinyl covering on it. He reached for the glass of Tropicana orange juice. His mother had put it on the table for him. He extended his arm. He knocked the juice glass clear across the table. It spilled onto the floor. A glass pitcher of Maine's Finest maple syrup also went flying. He started laughing. His mother was standing at the avocado G.E. electric stove. She was dishing pancakes from the iron frying pan. She was putting them on a dish. She held her tongue. She put the porcelain dish piled with pancakes in front of her son. She went to the matching avocado G.E. refrigerator. She got the container of juice. She also fetched the bottle of syrup. She served her son his breakfast. She began mopping up the sticky mess. He had created the mess.

The phone on the oak desk in the Bush's Texas ranch rang. It was Daddy Bush. "Bar - gotta go to Houston tonight to put a deal together," the young father told his wife.

"Oh, great," Barbara replied. She was holding Robin in her arms. She was wiping cereal from the little girls' face. "I'm gonna need some help George. Googen is acting up again."

"OK," Poppy replied. "Do whatever you have to. Gotta run. Talk to you tonight."

"Mummsy," young George yelled. He was in the front foyer. He threw on his yellow rain slicker. He was ready for school. "I can't find my pencil case," he cried.

"You had it last night. It was in your room," his mother yelled back. "Check there."

Young George found his pencil box. It was under his bed. "I've got it, Mummsy," he yelled. Then he fired up his train set. He lay on the floor. He was making loud choo-choo sounds.

"Georgie," his mother yelled. "You're gonna be late. It's your first day of school."

"OK Mummsy," he said. "Coming."

His mother sighed heavily. She whispered to Robin, "Don't you be like your big brother. You be a good girl for your mama."

Georgie had been attending kindergarten at Sam Houston Elementary School for two weeks. His teacher, Olive Barnes, called the Bush house. Barbara answered.

"Mrs. Bush? I'm Olive Barnes, George's teacher," Barns said. "George was throwing paper airplanes in class. One of them hit one of the girls in the face. I would appreciate it if you would talk to him."

"Oh my lord," Barbara sighed. "OK. Thank you for letting me know."

It was one thing after another with George Walker Bush. This was in the days before parents began pouring mood-enhancing drugs down their children's throats. If a kid was overactive, he was overactive. As a parent, you just dealt with it. You did the best you could.

It was May 1952. Her husband's oil career was blossoming. Barbara was pregnant again.

She was dying for another girl. She loved her Georgie. Robin was more her speed. Robin was easy to get along with. She was never the out-of-control kid her brother had always been. Georgie had been a handful since he came home from the hospital. Her husband was also hankering for another daughter. He was rarely home. He infrequently took on the parenting chores. Yet he thought it would be nice to have another girl.

The four Bushes packed up the family. They headed for Kennebunkport. That was where George Herbert Walker Bush's uncle had built a huge home along the water's edge. The property fronted on Ocean Avenue. Typically the Bush family would open up the summer cottage on Memorial Day weekend. The Bushes flew from Houston to New York. From there they flew on to Portland, Maine. In Portland, relatives picked them up at the airport. They drove them to down to

the family compound. It was an old stone-and-shingle mansion overlooking the Atlantic. It was a breathtaking spot. Any
child would be blessed to have such a summer playground.

They arrived at the house. Georgie jumped from the car. He
ran across the front yard. He got to a rock wall. The wall en-
circled the street side of the house. It was along the harbor.
The tide was out. It was a 30-foot drop to the ocean's edge.
Young George was kneeling on the wall. He was trying to see
if he could see any fish. That's when his mother eyed his pre-
carious perch.

"Honey," she yelled. "Get back from the edge." She asked
her husband to go rescue his son. But he had his hands full.
He had fishing tackle and poles. He had been preparing for an
outing with his Biddeford fishing buddy, Bob Boilard.

"Can you get him?" her husband asked her. "I'm already
late for my fishing date."

Barbara rolled her eyes. This was not only life in Texas.
This was life also in Maine. This was life no matter where they
were. Barbara was saddled with the parenting work. She her
husband flitted about with whatever diversion he could find.
And in Kennebunkport, it was even harder for her. She was in
the company of her in-laws. In fact, her father-in-law,
Prescott Bush, was in the throes of a campaign for the U.S.
Senate. So the family was quite busy. They were making sure
the family matriarch won the biggest political prize any of
them would have ever known.

His father was out fishing. Young George decided to go
down to the edge of the water. He was on the back side of the
house. He was barefoot. He walked on the rocks. He headed
toward the water. He slipped and fell. He landed on a piece of
sharp broken glass. His right knee began gushing gobs of
blood. He started screaming. His mother was gardening with
Robin. She dropped everything. She came running. She
scooped him up. She took him inside the house. Her father-
in-law was in the den. He was meeting with his political advisors. They were helping him with his Senate campaign.

"Can you take him into the other room?" Prescott Bush
asked his daughter-in-law. He was referring to his injured
grandson. "We're meeting here and need quiet."

Barbara was stunned. But then again, she wasn't. Prescott
Bush was his son's father. They were both cut from the same
cloth. She tended to her son's knee. She cleansed it with

witch hazel and wrapped it with fresh white gauze from a first-aid kit. The kit was always ready to go by the rear door of the house. The house opened onto the beach.

Barbara Bush had grown up with every little girl's wish. It was to get married and raise a family. She was quickly coming to realize she had married a cold blueblood. His priorities were money, fishing and golf. Not necessarily in that order. And who could blame him? He'd survived an ill-fated combat mission. His crewmates had died in that crash. The way George Herbert Walker looked at things, he was due some good time. Of course, he was also conflicted by his stern father's expectations for him. He had to at least put on a face of working hard. To a degree he did. In the early 1950s he co-founded the Bush-Overbey Oil Development Co. in Midland, Texas. His co-founder was John Overbey.

In November 1952, Prescott Bush was elected to the U.S. Senate. Biographer Herbert S. Parmet described him as "intimidating." Prescott Bush was now a member of the power structure in the nation's capital. He would continue to set an unreachable tone for his son and for his grandchildren.

George H.W. Bush's oil-development company was growing. So too was his young family.

On Feb. 11, 1953, Barbara Bush was home when she went into labor. She called the local fire department. An ambulance was dispatched. Paramedics found her alone at home. She was sitting on the floor. She was next to her bed. She was sweating profusely and moaning. She had tried to call her husband. But his secretary told Barbara he was out at his weekly Rotary Club luncheon. He couldn't be reached by phone. The two paramedics came to Barbara's aid. They lifted her onto a gurney. They wheeled her out the front door of the Bush's home. They gingerly lifted the gurney and pregnant woman into the back of their rig. They rushed to Presbyterian Medical Center in Midland. She was admitted to the maternity ward. She was alone. Nurses began preparing her for delivery. H. Her husband rushed in. He ran to her side grabbed her hand. "Oh, thank goodness," she told him. "I was worried you wouldn't get here."

"Oh, I wouldn't miss this," her husband replied. "Sorry I didn't get to you sooner. Rotary ran late."

At 2:03 p.m. Barbara gave birth to John Ellis Bush. He came to be known by family and friends as "Jeb." Jeb was an acronym representing his three initials. He had his mother's face. He was more a Pierce than a Bush. He didn't look like Googen. Googen more closely resembled his father. Robin was more of a cross between her two parents. She had her Mommy's eyes. She had her Daddy's elongated facial structure.

After Jeb was born, Barbara spent two days at Presbyterian. Her husband had hired a local nanny. He figured she would help keep things under control at their home. The nanny was Brooke Logan. She was a local college student. She picked up Googen at school while his mother was convalescing. Barbara got home with her new baby son. Young George and Robin were in the kitchen. They were with Brooke. They were having an after-school snack.

"Hi Mummsy," Georgie yelled. Barbara came in the front door holding her new baby. Young George ran up to his mother. He gave her a big hug. He nearly smothered his new little brother.

Parmet was a professor of history emeritus at the City University of New York. He described in his biography of George H.W. Bush the turn of events surrounding Robin:

"Jeb had just been born when, early in the spring of 1953, 3-year-old Robin woke up pale and lethargic. The small bruises on her legs had gone unnoticed, but the child's listlessness told Barbara something was wrong. She took her to the pediatrician, Dr. Dorothy Wyvell. After testing Robin's blood, the doctor asked Barbara to return that afternoon with her husband. Bush, who was doing some work at the courthouse over in the next county, rushed back. Dr. Wyvell explained that Robin had advanced leukemia. It had probably developed while they were still in California. The doctor had never seen a while blood cell count that high. The Bushes had many friends by then, and although Dr. Wyvell had advised that nobody be told since Robin had only about three weeks to live, word got around quickly...

George and Barbara ignored Dr. Wyvell's opinion that Robin's case was hopeless. They flew her to New York the next morning. Dr. John Walker, president of New York's Sloan-Kettering Memorial Hospital, was also George's uncle. He suggested that she be examined by Sloan-Kettering Foundations specialists. They gave the child a new cancer drug, which seemed to work, but not fully.

Robin held on for seven months. When she seemed well, they spent the time in Midland, but there were long days in New York. They moved into a relative's Sutton Place apartment so that Barbara could be at Robin's bedside every day. George had to return to work but flew back to New York on weekends. He left his two boys with neighbors until his mother sent a nurse to Texas to help. He drew whatever comfort he could from daily prayers in his church and by immersing himself in his work. The immediate burden of caring for Robin fell to Barbara, who was then only twenty-eight. It was at that time that her hair began to turn gray.

In October, while George was on his way back to her bedside, Robin began to hemorrhage. The Sloan-Kettering doctors decided to operate, but she didn't survive the surgery, and died before her father could get there."

Robin's older brother, George Walker Bush, took on pangs of guilt over his baby sister's unexpected death. He thought he might have done something to cause it. After all, he was only a child himself. But he seemed to grow into a man's body the day he heard that his little sister had passed away. "Mommy, why do you look so sad?" He asked his mother as she sat down in the edge of his bunk bed in their Midland home. She was about to read a book to her older son. She had put down Jeb for his nap.

"Honey," Barbara told George, "don't worry about me. You just be a good little boy. You make your Mommy and Daddy proud." She gave Georgie a hug. She started reading to him.

It was late April 1954. Young George woke up to the sound of a heavy Texas rainstorm on the roof of their small house. He lay in bed. He stared at the ceiling. This little boy had never been so reflective. "I need Mommy to be happy," he told himself. He whipped off the covers. He jumped out of bed. He raced into his parents' bedroom. "Hey Mummsy!" he shouted. He jumped on top of his mother. She was still sleeping. "Get up, Mummsy! It's time for pancakes! Come on Mommy. Wake up!"

Barbara opened her eyes to this startling Saturday morning greeting. She looked over. She noticed that her husband was gone. He had gotten up early. He had made himself coffee. He had left to play golf. Despite the rain, he was hoping against hope that the skies would clear. And even if they didn't, he could spend some time with the guys at the club. He would try to assuage some of the deep sadness he was feeling over the loss of his little Robin.

They had lost their Robin some eight months ago. It was now late May. It was time for George and Barbara Bush to prepare for their annual spring trip to Maine. Each year, the ritual was prescribed. The Bush clan would meet at Kennebunkport on Memorial Day weekend. They would open up the cottage. They would begin the summer solstice. This year would be hard. They were going to Maine without their Robin. But the Bushes relied on faith and friends. That would hold them together. And young George. The cutup he had become, was always there for some comedic relief. He was nearly 6 years old now. His little brother, Jeb, was now about 15 months old. George was the fidgety one. Jeb was much quieter. They were two different children. George was wiry. He would rarely sit still. Jeb was a less excitable sort. George was as skinny as a string bean. His little brother was chubby. George enjoyed being around his little brother. He considered him a toy. Their mother was always on the lookout for Jeb. She feared that his older brother would end up doing something foolish with his baby brother. That could endanger both boys. On this day, Georgie had grabbed a set of blocks from his closet. He was trying to balance them on Jeb's head. Suddenly the blocks fell onto the floor. One of them struck Jeb's nose. It triggered a trail of wails from little Jeb. Barbara came running.

"George, you give your brother a hug and tell him you are sorry," she told her older son.

"Sorry Jebbie," George told his brother. He gave him a bear hug. He then ran out of the room. He needed to use the bathroom.

These boys were not just any boys. They were now the grandsons of a United States senator. Their grandfather was Prescott Bush. He had by now served roughly more than a year of his Senate term. Their grandfather was the patriarch of the growing Bush clan. He was hoping that his son George Herbert Walker Bush would someday follow in his political footsteps. But Prescott sensed that his older grandson, George Walker Bush, might need a father who could devote more time to keeping his son on the straight and narrow. Better that than an absentee father whose interest in politics would come first. "I hope Georgie can slow down," Prescott once said to his wife, Dorothy, the boy's grandmother. "I don't know what it is with that boy. He's a handful."

By this time, George H.W. Bush's career in the oil business was on the fast track. In 1953, he had co-founded Zapata Petroleum in Midland, Texas. His co-founders were Hugh and Bill Liedtke. He wrote to his father the senator. He told him he had run in to a senator from Texas. He had run into Lyndon Johnson in Midland. He reported that Johnson described Prescott's election as "'the best thing that happened to the 83rd Congress.' "

If such correspondence helped endear son to father, it also would begin setting a foundation for George H.W. Bush's growing interest in politics.

One day he was meeting with the Liedtke brothers in his Midland office. Bush's phone rang. "Your son is on the line," Bush's secretary, Judith Doble, told him.

"OK, put him through," Bush told her.

"Daddy! Will you come home so we can play?" Georgie asked his father.

"I can't right now," his father told him. "We'll play later." Bush hung up the phone.

His son was crestfallen. He wondered why he never got to play with his Daddy.

"Mommy, let's play," Georgie said to his mother. "Daddy doesn't want to."

"OK honey," his mother said. "Daddy will be home later."

Chapter III
Bad Jeans

Junior was how some people came to call George W. Bush.

He was sitting in Room 233 at Phillips Andover Academy. His parents had sent him to prep school to knock some sense into him. They remained back in Houston. Andover was also George H.W. Bush's alma mater. He and his wife hoped it would help straitjacket their mischievous son.

It was his freshman year. George was now a young teenager. He had moved on from middle school to high school. He was sitting near the rear of the room. His homeroom teacher was John Brochu. Brochu began taking attendance. George took a rubber band from the left front pocket of his khaki chinos. He stretched it between the thumb and forefinger of his right hand. Mr. Brochu looked down at the class list for the next name. A loud snap broke the silence. The paperclip shot from George's hand like a bullet. It hit the blackboard in front of the room. Blood suddenly oozed from Mr. Brochu's left temple.

"Ouch!" the teacher yelled. He reached up with his right hand. He rubbed his temple with his middle finger. He took his finger from his head and looked at it. He saw blood. He pulled a silk white handkerchief from his pocket. He held it against his temple. The class broke out in laughter. These were young teenagers. They knew from instinct what had happened. But they weren't sure who had fired the paperclip. George tried to put the rubber band back into his pocket. He hoped no one would see who pulled off this prank. It snapped by a mistake. All eyes turned to George. Now the culprit had been seen.

Brochu was a short, stout man. He saw himself as Andover's law-and-order man. He had now figured out what had happened. He figured out who had done it. There were twitters and laughter from the other students in the room. Brochu walked over to George's desk. "Young man, I could see through your head with a flashlight," Brochu cracked.

But the young Bush had a reply ready. "Mr. Brochu, I could see through your head without a flashlight," he told the teacher.

Brochu wasn't amused. George's classmates were. They roared in approval. Brochu was red in the face. He grabbed George's arm. He marched him to Headmaster John Hart's office.

Hart was a kindly man. He had a good sense of humor. He told Brochu, "I'll take care of it." Hart sat George down in his office. He chatted with the boy. Hart wanted to know why someone would act out like this. He was more interested in preventing another episode. He also wanted to make sure this would become a lesson on the path to a boy's maturity. He didn't want simply an excuse to mete out punishment.

"I was just having some fun," George told the headmaster. He tried to explain his behavior.

"OK, George but you need to understand that what you did was not only potentially dangerous. It also disrupted Mr. Brochu's attempts to prepare the class for the rest of the year," Hart told him. Hart also told George to consider this a warning. Such behavior wouldn't be tolerated again. The headmaster made a note in George's student file. He mailed a note home to George's parents. George said he understood that he had done something wrong. He shook Mr. Hart's hand. He walked out of the headmaster's office. He headed for the library.

"Hey Junior," said his friend, Will Hemingway. Hemingway ran in to his buddy in the main lobby just outside the headmaster's office. "What's up?"

"Not much big boy," George W. replied. "Same old shit. Hey, let's hit the package store. I need me a cold one baby."

"Great idea, Junior," Hemingway replied. They figured they'd sneak out of school. They'd head downtown to see if they could find someone who could vouch for them. They were underage and not old enough to buy alcohol. With help they could pick up a couple of six-packs.

The two boys would be skipping Latin class. Their Latin teacher was Audrey Meader. She was a shapely young teacher. Many of the boys at Andover had a crush on her. She was 21. She wasn't that much older than most of her students. Bush and Hemingway rarely found an excuse to skip Miss Meader's class. They rarely found an excuse to skip any class. Bush told his pal he was in no mood today to sit through a Latin lecture. Miss Meader or no Miss Meader.

"Willy," Bush said to Hemingway. He threw some books in his hallway locker. "Let's get the hell out of here. Someone's gonna ask us what why we're not in class."

"Hey, Junior," Hemingway whispered, "keep it down. I just spotted Mr. Hart doing hallway checks." If they ran into John Hart, their headmaster, there would be trouble. It's the last thing George Bush needed right now. He had just gotten into trouble with the rubber band and paper clip in Mr. Brochu's homeroom. The boys slipped outside a side door in Building "C." They successfully avoided having to pass by the head office. The head office was in the main building on campus. They walked toward the bus stop on Catherine Street. They figured they might catch a bus before they could hitch a ride by thumbing. They got to the bus stop. A Metro bus headed downtown was pulling in. A passenger got off. Just the luck the boys needed. They hopped on board. Young Bush realized he didn't have any change.

"Hey, Will, can you spot me a dime?" Hemingway put two dimes in the cash box. The cash box was next to the driver. The boys took a seat in the middle of the bus.

"Junior, how the hell are we gonna buy beer if you don't have any money?" Hemingway asked.

"Don't worry, Willie Boy," Bush responded. "Hey one more thing - kiss my ass."

Hemingway laughed. That was George W. Bush's affect on people. He made them laugh. Life of the party. That's why they liked being around him. Whether or not he ever had any money for beer didn't matter.

The boys got off at the first stop in downtown Andover. It was just a block from a nearby package store. They walked into the parking lot outside C&M Liquors. They saw an old wino standing at the far corner of the building.

"Willie, follow me," Bush told Hemingway. Bush walked up to the old guy in the lot. The man was wearing a navy-blue knitted pullover cap. He had a scraggly gray beard. Most of his teeth were missing. His eyes were bloodshot. They were half closed. He was wearing a worn plaid flannel shirt. He had on greasy green uniform pants. He had worn rubber packs on his feet.

"How ya doin'?" Bush asked the man.

The man replied, "Hey you boys got a quarter I can borrow?" Bush saw an opportunity. They'd give this guy money for wine. In turn maybe he'd buy them some beer. What a deal.

"We need some beer," Bush told the man. "If you'll buy for us, we'll give you money for some wine."

"OK, the old guy said. "Gimme the money. What kinda beer you want?"

"Don't matter, whatever's cheap," Hemingway told the man. "Get us two six-packs."

Bush handed the man a ten-dollar bill. The boys waited outside. The man went inside for the loot. A few minutes later, the boys had their beer. The wino had his wine. Everybody was happy. The boys caught a bus back to campus. They went to their dorm. They proceeded to Bush's room. It was time to quench their thirst. Bush cracked open his first can. He fetched a pack of cigarettes - Camel straights - from his dresser drawer. "Hey Willie Boy, here ya go," Bush said. He tossed his friend a butt.

"Hey, thanks, butt boy," Hemingway said. He was laughing.

"Hey Willie Boy, kiss my ass," Bush shot back. He pulled a wooden match from the breast pocket of his pink Hathaway oxford shirt. He swiped it across the sole of his Bass Weejuns. The boys sat back. They enjoyed their beer and cigarettes.

"Willie Boy," Bush said. "Wanna rob a bank?"

"Jeezus," Hemingway said. "What are you Junior, nuts?"

"Come on Willie," W said. "No balls, no glory."

After a few more beers, the boys fell asleep. Bush's robbery plans were on hold. They awoke a few hours later. W was on the floor beneath his desk. It was now 6:45 p.m.. It was just 15 minutes before the dining hall would stop serving dinner.

"Willie, let's get goin'," Bush said. "We've only got a few minutes to get some grub."

The boys tossed their empties into a laundry bag. They threw it in to the closet. They knew enough to keep the empties out of sight. Otherwise the resident advisor, Jim Thorpe, might walk into the room. He would see what the boys had been doing. W and Hemingway closed the door of the room. They jogged to Simpson Dining Hall. They walked in through the front glass doors. They passed a vending machine.

"Hold on," W said suddenly. He dug his hand in his pocket for some change. He pulled out a quarter. He inserted it into the machine. He pulled the lever. Out came a Devil Dog. "Hey, check this out," he laughed. He held the elongated Devil Dog in front of the fly on his beige chinos.

"In your dreams," Hemingway replied. He was laughing. They walked up to the food line. They were the last two students in line.

W saw the dining-room attendant behind the stainless steam table. He told her he'd like the sloppy Joes. "Some fries, too," he ordered. Hemingway opted for pork chops. They handed their meal cards to the attendant at the end of the line. She punched the cards. The boys took their trays over to a table by a window. The window overlooked the campus green.

Hemingway went to sit down. W quickly pulled the Devil Dog from his pants pocket. He tossed it on the chair Hemingway was about to sit in. Hemingway sat down. He squashed the Devil Dog. The impact broke open the cellophane wrapping. The seat of his pants was now covered with a squashed Devil Dog. W played a straight face.

"You're an asshole,' Hemingway told him. Bush laughed. He took a salt shaker from the table. He poured some salt onto Hemingway's pork chops. This was a guy who was tough to dislike. It didn't matter how much of a pain in the ass he could be.

W suddenly began feeling nauseous. The effect of the beers was overwhelming his empty stomach. He started retching. He made a beeline for the bathroom. In the nick of time he reached the rest room. He ran up to a sink. He dropped his head. He started vomiting. He ran some cold water. He splashed it in his face. He grabbed some paper towels. He cleaned up. He went back to the dinner table. He pushed his tray away. He asked Hemingway, "Finished? Let's blow this joint." They walked back to their respective dorms. Tomorrow would be another day. Hangover or no hangover.

The sun was shining brightly in through the window of the old, white Victorian mansion. It was Junior's dorm. It was shortly after 7 a.m. Bush awoke. He had a throbbing, aching headache. He put both hands on his head. He closed his eyes. He tried to will away the pain. He couldn't remember what day it was. Would he have to go to class? Or was this a Saturday? He had to go to the bathroom badly. He tried to get up from bed. He fell back down. He couldn't get up to steady himself. He lay down. He closed his eyes. He begged for the headache and nausea to go away.

"Hey Junior," he suddenly heard someone say. "Wanna drink?"

Bush recognized Hemingway's voice. Hemingway was at the door of his room.

"Don't say the word 'drink,'" Bush told his buddy. "God help me."

Hemingway wasn't feeling well himself. But he'd had only five of the beers. Bush had drunk seven. Hemingway came in to W's room. He sat down in an old overstuffed chair. He quickly dozed off. The two of them awoke. It was already 10:30 a.m. Bush ran to the bathroom down the hall. He raced to the toilet. He got on his knees. He began retching. He was vomiting. Sloppy Joe's and cheap beer.

It wasn't pretty.

"Somebody help me," he yelled. He was now shivering uncontrollably. He was drenched in perspiration. He slumped to the cold, white-tiled floor. He curled into a fetal position. He closed his eyes. He stayed there for more than an hour. It was now a bit before noon. Junior slowly tried to stand up. He couldn't. He dragged himself across the tile floor. He made it to the stall shower. He reached up to turn on the water. He was now underneath a spigot of icy cold water. He sat here for 15 minutes. He finally decided he was so cold he couldn't stand it any longer. He reached up. He turned on the hot spigot. He sat on the shower floor another 15 minutes. He was beneath a torrent of refreshment.

"Never again," he said to himself. He referred to the drinking binge. Famous last words. He'd repeated them too many times.

Bush hadn't brought a towel to the bathroom with him. He reached up to turn off the hot- and cold-water faucets. He was still on the floor of the shower. He was still shivering. He hadn't brought a towel to the bathroom with him. But he knew he had to get out of the shower. He had to get back to his room to get a towel. Otherwise he would shiver to death. He slowly tried to stand up to leave the shower. He suddenly felt dizzy. He couldn't stand up. He fell to the wet, cold tile floor of the shower. The bathroom door opened.

"Junior?"

It was Hemingway. He was looking for his friend Bush.

"I'm in here," Bush muttered. Hemingway came over and put his hands under Bush's arms. He tried to lift him up. Bush had no energy to stand up. He was dead weight. Hemingway dragged him from the shower to the bathroom door. He pried open the door with his foot. He dragged Bush down the hall to his room. He put Bush alongside the bed. He reached to a nearby desk chair. He grabbed a bath towel. He covered Bush with. Bush was shivering. He was whimpering.

Hemingway was the kind of friend anyone needs. He walked to basement of the house. A found the soda machine. He dropped a quarter in the slot. He punched the button for a Coca-Cola. He sprinted to W's room. He snapped the top of the bottle on the edge of the desk. The cap snapped off. He kneeled. He handed it to Bush. Bush was virtually lifeless. He couldn't use his arms. Hemingway held the lip of the bottle to Bush's mouth. He tipped it ever-so-slightly. Some soda dribbled into Bush's mouth.

Junior was moaning. "Ohhhhhhhhhhhhhh....." His moans drifted off. His eyes were barely open. He was dehydrated.

Hemingway continued to administer the drops of Coke on to Bush's lips. Anything to start getting some fluids in to him. "George, bear with me," Hemingway told him. "Keep on truckin'. You're gettin' there."

Bush's drinking prowess wasn't what he wished. But is anyone's, ever? Over-consumption of the wicked alcohol has the same effect on everybody. Drink too much and the body toxifies. The liver can't process an excess of liquor. It becomes overwhelmed. There is no turning back.

George fell asleep. It was mid-afternoon by the time he had enough energy to raise himself from the bed. He was shaking and pale. He tried to stand on his feet. His head was throbbing. H could barely stay on his feet. He stumbled to the door of his room. He banged in to the door jam. He tried to get to the bathroom. He grabbed the jam with his right hand. He tried to keep himself upright. He was barely able to make it down the hall to the bathroom. He finally made it to one of the urinals. He stood in front of the urinal. He put his left hand on the wall to prop himself up. He unzipped his fly with his right hand. He urinated. He rested his head on the wall above the urinal. After urinating, he didn't have the energy to zip up his fly. His eyes were still half-shut. He was still feeling woozy. He slowly made his way back to his room. He fell into bed. He collapsed. He was comatose. Hemingway covered him with a blanket.

"George, I'll be in my room," Hemingway told him.

"Screw you," Bush replied. That was an indication to Hemingway that he was actually starting to get back his sense of humor. He was mending from the drinking binge. Time was healing the pain. Slowly but surely.

Bush slept for nearly 17 hours. He awoke just before 7 a.m. the next day. "Come on Junior, we gotta go to class," Hemingway said. He burst through the door. "We're in deep shit if we don't show up for chemistry. Mr. Vuley will kill us. Come on shithead."

"Screw off," Junior shot back. "Hey Willie, kiss my ass. Did you bring me some coffee?"

"Come on George, we'll hit the dining hall on the way and get some. Let's go. Now," Hemingway demanded.

Bush pulled himself together. He was dehydrated. But the nausea had abated. He walked to the bathroom. He turned on the cold water in the sink. He reached down with both hands. He cupped his palms. He brought handfuls of cold water to his parched face. It felt heavenly. He grabbed some paper towels. He wiped his face. He walked back to the room. He threw on some pants, a shirt and his loafers. "Hey Willie," he said, "I need a beer."

"Not on your life," Hemingway said. He was laughing in amazement. "Maybe later, though. I could use one too."

"One?" Junior asked. "How about a dozen?"

In her Houston home, meanwhile, Barbara Bush was sitting at her kitchen desk. She was organizing the household bills. She wrote several checks. She licked the postage stamps for the envelopes. She prepared to leave them at the front door. From there the mailman could take them when he arrived with the Bush's daily mail. She opened the door. She saw the mailman. He was walking up the brick walkway.

"Hello Mrs. Bush," said Peter Colt. Colt was mail carrier the Bush's were quite friendly with.

"Hi Peter," Barbara Bush replied. Colt handed Mrs. Bush a sheaf of mail. She in turn gave him three stamped envelopes containing checks.

"Thanks much Peter," she said.

"OK, ma'am, my pleasure," Colt replied. "We'll see you soon."

Colt left the house. Mrs. Bush went inside. She began reviewing her mail. She was at her desk. Among the items was an envelope with a Massachusetts postmark. It was from Andover. Mrs. Bush picked up her sterling letter opener. It was an heirloom. It came from her mother. It still had an engraved "P" on the handle. Her maiden name was Pierce. She opened the envelope. She unfolded what appeared to be a letterhead from the school. Andover. George W. Bush was back in New England. The letter was from the headmaster's office. It was addressed to "Mr. and Mrs. George H.W. Bush."

"Please be advised that, due to an incident in which your son, George W. Bush, was involved in his assigned home room, a warning has been placed in his student file." The very impersonal letter went on to explain that the Bush's oldest son had pulled a prank in school. It involved a rubber band and a paperclip. It had slightly injured a teacher in Junior's home room.

"We will keep this warning on file," Hart said in his letter. "If within the next year your son is involved in any additional untoward behavior, disciplinary action will be considered by the Board of Directors. Under our policy, it can entail anything from a second warning to a five-day suspension. Please contact me if you have any concerns or questions. Best, John Hart, Headmaster." His signature appeared above his typewritten name and title.

Barbara Bush slowly placed the letter on her desk. She looked up. She stared in to space. She bowed her head. She lifted her hands. She cupped her face. She had hoped that Andover would help straighten out her troublesome boy. Now she was wondering. Would even prep school be the answer? Would it ensure that the man who bore the George Bush name would be able to carry the heavy mantle as the progeny of a United States senator? Tears welled in her eyes.

"I need to tell George," she thought to herself. She referred to her husband.

Simply for Barbara Bush to repeat the thought to herself was odd. Of course she had to tell her husband. What she really was wondering was what his reaction would be. More to the point, would he care enough? Would he even want to discuss how to help their eldest child? Could they stop whatever was triggering the aberrant behavior that now was affecting his schooling? She didn't even know yet about his drinking. Or, if she knew or suspected it was going on, she chose to somehow bury it within her psyche.

By now, "Junior" had two more brothers. Neil Mallon Bush was born in Midland, Texas, in 1955. Marvin Pierce Bush came into the world the following year. He was also a Midland native. A second sister, Dorothy Ellis Bush, was born in Houston in 1959.

The family was pinning its legacy on the eldest child. Prescott Bush wanted to see George W. Bush carry on the name.

The phone rang. "Hello?" Barbara Bush said. She picked up the wall phone. She was in her kitchen.

"It's me," said her husband. "Thought you'd like to know we just hit it big with a deal. We got a contract for some new fields. They might have some rich veins in them."

Barbara Bush feigned excitement. "Oh, great honey," she replied.

"Yeah," her husband said. "It's a good gig. What's going there?"

"Oh, not much," Barbara responded. She would have brought up the letter had her husband sensed something was going on with her. She found it easier to let it be for now.

"OK," her husband said. "I'll see ya later. Probably be home about 6. Gotta go sign these contracts later. Might stop by the club for a victory drink on the way home."

"OK," Barbara said. "Bye, bye."

Barbara hung up the phone. She picked up Hart's letter and refolded it. She placed it back in the envelope. She ran her right forefinger and thumb along the bottom crease of the envelope. She placed it just above her desk in her "in" slot. She walked over to the stove. She picked up the white porcelain teapot. She took it to the sink. She drew some cold water. She placed the teapot on the right front burner. She turned the knob to "high." She stood before the stove. She waited for the water to boil. She was trancelike. She was sick. She was worried about George W. Bush. He was the boy who was her morale-booster. She knew who had gotten her through Robin's illness. She knew who had gotten her through Robin's death. It was Junior. Junior had somehow sensed he was the one who needed to keep his mother strong.

Junior and Hemingway ran into the dining hall. They wanted to grab some coffee. They were already running late for chemistry class. That was par for the course. W grabbed a paper cup. He placed it on the counter next to a pot of coffee. The dining-hall attendants had brewed it earlier. He poured himself a cup of coffee. He placed the pot back on the stainless Bunn hotplate.

"Willie, want some Joe?" he asked Hemingway.

"Yeah," his friend replied. "Do bears shit in the woods?"

W, never to be outsmarted, said, "Kiss my ass. You want cream in that?"

"Yeah," Hemingway replied.

"OK," W said. "Cream in your jeans." He tossed a small plastic container of creamer to Hemingway. The two left the dining hall. They headed for class. They walked across the green. They entered the steel-and-glass Life Sciences Building. They took the elevator to the second floor. They walked in to Mr. Vuley's classroom. It was 8:13 a.m. They were 13 minutes late. Vuley had already begun his lecture. He was in front of the classroom. He was at the chalkboard. He was explaining the element table. He glanced to his right. He saw the two boys saunter in to his class. He noticed they were late. He was not one to seek a confrontation. He looked at the boys. He kept on with his lecture. The boys went to the back of the room. They found two available seats. Seated between them was Martha Hamilton. She was a blond girl from a wealthy family in Concord, Mass. Untold numbers of other boys in school thought Martha was the cat's meow. So did W. Besides her beauty, Martha was sweet. She was very intelligent.

W pulled from his left front pant's pocket a creamer. He had taken it from the dining hall. He got Hamilton's attention. He held up the creamer. He was smiling. He said nothing. She said nothing. He smiled at her. He put the creamer on his desk.

"Mr. Bush, how many of the 106 known elements occur naturally in nature," Vuley suddenly asked. Vuley turned from the chalkboard to face the class.

Bush had been thinking of a way to make Martha Hamilton laugh. He looked up. He was surprised by the question. "Uh, let's see...88?" Bush replied.

"OK," Vuley said. He approved the answer. "We're glad you could be here today. You too, Mr. Hemingway."

Vuley turned back to the chalkboard. Bush suddenly tossed the creamer to Hemingway. The creamer was warm and soggy by now. It dripped all over the top of Hamilton's desk. It ruined the notes she was taking. "Sorry," W whispered to her. "I'll settle up with you after."

Hamilton was quite unimpressed. She liked Bush. She thought he was funny. She thought he was cute. But she was mad that he got her desk full of warm cream.

Hemingway got wet as he caught the creamer. He was simply trying to make sure Vuley didn't see the boys screwing off in class. He quickly stuck the soggy creamer in his pants pocket.

"Lab has been rescheduled," Vuley told his class. The hour was ending. "We'll meet in "B" lab Friday instead of "A" lab. The bell rang for classes to change. Vuley said, "Mr. Bush and Mr. Hemingway. Please stop to see me on the way out."

W. looked at his buddy Hemingway. He smirked. "Now the shit hits the fan," W told Hemingway. Here we go again."

The students in front of them filed out of the room. W and Hemingway stayed behind. They approached Mr. Vuley. He was erasing the blackboard.

"Gentlemen," Vuley said, I need you to be here on time. It does you no good to miss lecture. It also disrupts the rest of the class when you stroll in here late."

"Yeah, OK bud," Bush told the teacher. Hemingway simply nodded in acknowledgment. The two boys walked out the door of the classroom. They headed into the hallway. W was scheduled next period for a study hall. Hemingway was up for a biology lecture. "Willie boy, catch you later," W told Hemingway.

Bush made his way to study hall. He passed by the Student Union. He decided to run in. He figured he'd grab a soda. He was still feeling quite parched from the drinking binge with his buddy. A cold Coke sure would hit the spot. He ran up the concrete steps of the stone, ivy-covered building. He pulled open the huge oak door at the entrance. Martha Hamilton was on her way out.

"Hey Mar," Bush said excitedly. "Can I buy you a drink?"

"George, it's the middle of the day," she told him.

"No, uh, I mean a Coke, chick," he said. "Too early for a brewskie." He had a reputation as a party boy. He didn't need an excuse to find a good, cold beer. His reputation was far and wide on the Andover campus.

Bushie was a cut-up. His education came second. That's how he saw his purpose at Andover. His first priority was having a good time.

"Thanks, but I'll pass," Hamilton told him. "Ah, jeez, Mar, come on. Be a sport." She liked W. But she took a pass.

"Thanks, but really, I need to get to English," she said. She passed by him. She went through the door.

"That's cool," Bush said. "Later, chickie."

She wasn't hot on the "chickie" thing. But Bush was Bush. She was slightly offended at the condescending reference to her gender. Hamilton alternately, secretly enjoyed Bush's light-hearted approach to life.

Bush skipped down the winding wooden stairway. He headed to the basement. He found two vending machines along the wall. He dug his right hand into his pocket. He found two dimes and a nickel. He put in the coin slot of the soda machine. He pulled the chrome lever for a Coke. With a bang a bottle of the great elixir dropped down in to the wide opening toward the bottom of the machine. Bush stuck in his left hand. He grabbed the bottle. He stuck the top in the machine's bottle opener. He yanked with a downward motion. Bingo. He took a swig of the cold soda. He swished it around in his dry mouth. He swallowed. He felt like a new man. The cold effervescence traveled down his throat to his stomach. The only way it could have tasted better were if it had been a cold beer. Bush made his way back upstairs. He went out the front door. He walked next door to Douglas Hall. It was named for one of the school's founders. Frederick Douglas had been one of the school's original benefactors. He also shared a long-distant family connection to Bush ancestors.

Bush walked in to study hall. He saw a couple of empty desks in the second row of desks. Seated nearby was Edwin Forrester. Forrester was the son of a New York banker. Forrester and W had met at the freshman-class orientation. They had sat together and struck up a casual friendship. Forrester was a very studious sort. He was bookish. Bush was just the opposite. He was a happy-go-lucky kid. He never missed an opportunity to bring some levity to the fore. "Hey Eddie-baby," W said. "How's it hangin?"

Forrester was not accustomed to this kind of an informal, towel-snapping greeting. He kept a straight face. "Hello, George," Forrester replied. He extended his right hand to shake Bush's. Bush extended his hand in kind. He suddenly stuck up his thumb. He pulled away his hand. It was what jokesters do when someone else extends a hand. Forrester didn't know how to react. He seemed to enjoy someone who could be so irreverent. He also liked it that someone could be so comfortable in his irreverence.

Bush took a swig of his Coke. He swallowed loudly. He opened his mouth to make even more noise as he celebrated the moment.

"Mr. Bush, there are to be no beverages in classrooms," bellowed John McLaughlin. McLaughlin was a heavy-set math teacher. He was assigned as the study-hall monitor. "Please come forward and bring me the bottle."

Bush jumped. He pretended to be shocked at McLaughlin's sudden dressing down. Bush rose from his desk. He walked to the front of the room. He gave McLaughlin the bottle. But he grabbed two final, loud swigs from it. Why waste a Coke? "Here you go," Bush told McLaughlin. "There's a sip left for you in the bottom."

George W. Bush was never one to miss a chance for a wisecrack.

He returned to his seat. He smiled at Forrester. Forrester wasn't smiling. Forrester had his Latin book open. He looked up briefly merely to acknowledge Bush. He looked down at his book. Bush returned to his desk. Bush had one book with him from his U.S. history class. He opened it to page 53. Bush had marked the page with a bookmark - a Playboy magazine. He began browsing the Playboy. He turned to the centerfold. Bush tapped Forrester's left arm.

"Hey Treeman, check this out," Bush said to his seatmate. He used the nickname he had given Forrester. Forrester looked up to see the centerfold. He saw a nude model. He blushed. He quickly looked down again at his Latin book. Bush laughed. He continued his browsing. Study hall? No. Bush called it study hell. He couldn't be bothered with studying. Study hall had one purpose for him – entertainment. It was like anything else in his life. Look for the joy.

Bush browsed his Playboy. He kept one eye on the study-hall proctor, Mr. McLaughlin. He wanted to keep track of the teacher's whereabouts. He was keen to the notion that he wasn't supposed to be reading Playboy during study hall.

Perhaps the guilty look guilty. McLaughlin caught Bush's glance. The teacher sensed something was going on. He had been sitting at the desk in front of the room. He got up from his desk. He began walking around the room. He went up some of the aisles of desks. He got to the row of desks containing the one where Bush was sitting. McLaughlin started walking toward Bush. Bush suspected McLaughlin was headed over to his desk. He turned some pages in the history book. He wanted to mask the presence of the Playboy. McLaughlin got to Bush's desk. He stopped. He looked down at Bush. Bush looked up at McLaughlin.

"What's going on Junior?" McLaughlin asked Bushie.

"Can I get a pass to the rest room?" Bush asked him.

McLaughlin said, "Yeah, stop by my desk." Bush got up to follow McLaughlin to his desk. Bush picked up his history book. The Playboy was inside. He put it under his left arm. He got to McLaughlin's desk. He extended his right hand. He took the bathroom pass from McLaughlin.

"You don't need to bring your books to the bathroom," McLaughlin told him.

"Uh, good point," Bush replied. "Sorry I couldn't get it to you sooner." He returned to his desk briefly to drop the book. But now Bush had to follow through with his plans to use the bathroom. Otherwise McLaughlin would become suspicious. He walked out of the room. He headed toward the bathroom. McLaughlin went over to Bush's desk. He looked at the closed history book. He could tell its binding was stretched. He lifted the book slightly. He examined it more closely.

The teacher saw what he had suspected when Bush asked to go to the bathroom - with a book. McLaughlin could see that there was something inserted inside the history book. He was once an adolescent himself. He avoided speculation. Students over the years had done worse things at Andover. A little pleasure-reading inside one of their textbooks would hurt no one. McLaughlin might have even done it himself. He had attended the school in the 1950s. He chose not to examine the history book. He left it untouched in Bush's temporary absence. Instead, McLaughlin returned to his own desk in

front of the study hall. A few minutes passed. Bush re-
entered the study hall. He walked by the proctor's desk. Bush
placed the bathroom pass on McLaughlin's desk. He glanced
briefly at the teacher. He headed to his desk. Forty-three
minutes remained of study hall.

"Welcome back, Mr. Bush," McLaughlin said to him.

"Thanks," W replied. "Nice to be back."

McLaughlin added, "Now you can resume your history assignment."

Bush momentarily froze. He didn't know whether Mr.
McLaughlin had discovered that he'd placed some pleasure-
reading inside his history book. So, how to play it? Hope for
the best. Prepare for the worst. If McLaughlin asked about the
Playboy, Bush decided he would come clean. No harm in admitting an interest in naked women. So what if it could cost
you some detention time after school. Bush got to his desk.
He sat down. He glanced up. He looked guilty. He wanted to
see if McLaughlin was on to him. McLaughlin was looking
away. He was trying to avoid an uncomfortable moment. If
not the moment might grow in to a confrontation. Bush had
apparently dodged the bullet this time around. He spent a few
minutes reading about the United States' entry in to World
War II. The grandson of U.S. Sen. Prescott Bush had had
enough history. It was now time to check back with the
women gracing Hugh Hefner's famous magazine.

The bell rang. W was running his fingers over Miss October. It was time to change classes. Bushie was getting thirsty.
He was still suffering from the drinking binge with Will Hemingway. He was also developing a taste for alcohol.

Bush was scheduled for calculus lab. He found calculus a
bore. Calculus lab was even worse. His calculus teacher was
Lorraine Haynes. She was a purely and simply a bit fat
woman. Bush would laugh when she would talk to the students about calculus lab. He coined it calculus flab. Miss
Haynes was a kind-hearted, matronly spinster. Bush liked
her but he was bored.

He didn't want to sit in a stuffy, hot classroom. He didn't
want to catch up on his calculus homework. He started fig-
uring out how to get out of this alleged obligation. He walked
down the hall toward calc flab. He was about to pass a door
leading from Building D to a student-parking lot. He eyed the
door that stood between him and freedom. It was calc flab or

a bus ride downtown. Not much of a choice. He unassumingly walked straight out the door into the bright fall sunshine. He was afraid that someone of authority might see him outside. Bush was conscious of the fact that he needed to concentrate on getting off campus. Otherwise he would lose focus on the task at hand.

The guilty usually bring attention to themselves.

W headed for Providence Road. It was a small street running alongside the administration building at Andover. He crossed campus. He walked through a thicket of trees that populated the main green. He was getting thirstier by the minute. He got to Providence Road. He crossed the street. He headed to a small bus stop. It was a block away on Hillman Avenue. Within seconds he was at Hillman Avenue. He stood at the bus stop. He waited for the Metro bus. It would take him downtown.

"Hey Bushie!" Bush turned to the direction of the exclamation. He looked to his right. Across the street, diagonally. He saw Thorn McKenzie. Thorn was a boy from Greenwich, Conn. He was a junior at Andover. Thorn came from a wealthy family. It represented the majority stockholders in a national food conglomerate. Thorn enjoyed Bush. Bush was always up for a good laugh or prank. Anything to avoid the real issues.

"Hey Horney," Bush yelled. He was using the nickname he gave McKenzie.

McKenzie was holding a slew of books under his arm. He looked for traffic. He crossed Hillman Avenue to talk with W. "What's up," he asked Bush.

"It's Shits time," Bush said. He used his form of "Schlitz."

McKenzie seemed confused. Then he caught on to Ws lexicon. "I'm in," McKenzie said enthusiastically. The boys waited for the next bus.

Bushie pulled a mashed pack of Camel straights from his right front pocket. He managed with his left forefinger to get a squashed cigarette from the mangled pack. He stuck it between his lips. "Try wunna mine," he said to McKenzie. He extended his hand. He offered the pack of cigarettes to McKenzie.

"No thanks W," McKenzie replied. He was laughing. Bush pulled a wooden match from his left rear pocket. He swiped it across a steel upright. The upright helped support the 4-by-8-

foot outdoor bus shelter. He pulled the flame toward his mouth. He lighted his cigarette. He tossed the lighted match at McKenzie. He choked and laughed at the same time. He sucked in a mouthful of smoke. "You asshole," McKenzie said.

"Screw you," Bush replied. He took another drag on his Camel.

Bush saw a bus approaching. He took one final drag on his cigarette. He tossed it in a trash container next to the bus shelter.

"Hey idiot, you're gonna start a fire," McKenzie told Bush. He was half shocked. He was also envious. He wished he could be as daring and care-free as George W. Bush.

"Fire my ass," Bush shot back. The bus pulled up. The driver opened the door. "You headed downtown?" Bush asked the driver.

"Yeah," the driver replied. He avoided the reply he really wanted to come back with. (On all four sides of the bus were directional signs saying, "Downtown.")

"Cool," Bush replied. "Horney let's go."

McKenzie jumped onto the bus. Bush led the way. They placed change in the cash box next to the driver. They took seats near the front. The bus took on some more passengers. Bush observed the boredom by opening up his history book. There was Miss October again. She was waiting for him. That's how he saw it anyway. He began flipping through the Playboy.

"Hey W, nice," McKenzie said. He peered over Bush's arm at the magazine. "Can I?"

"Get your own, Horneyboy," Bush replied.

The bus approached the central Main Street stop. McKenzie stood up. He pulled the stop buzzer. Two more blocks later the bus came to a slow stop. The driver opened the front door. He also opened a side door near the middle of the vehicle.

"Thanks driverman," Bush said. He hopped off the bus.

"OK fellas," the driver said.

"We need someone to get us some brewskies," Bush told McKenzie. Bush looked around. He was trying to get his bearings. He looked toward the horizon to his left. He saw a familiar store. It was the Beverage Mart. It was an old prefabricated-metal warehouse that once served as a regional distribution center for Rossignol skis. Rossignol had since moved most of its operations west to Colorado. W knew the Beverage Mart. On previous occasions he had scored beer there.

"Come on Horney," he said to McKenzie. "Let's see what's up at Bev Fart. We'll see if we can find someone outside to buy for us." They crossed the street. They began walking over to the Beverage Mart. Bush had renamed it with a scatological bent. Bev Mart wasn't good enough. It had to be Bev Fart. They walked into the beverage center's parking lot. W and McKenzie began scoping the landscape for some help. A group of four people was standing outside smoking. They appeared to be of age. Maybe they were college kids. Bush saw a possible opportunity.

He walked ahead of McKenzie. He slowly approached the group. He saw two boys and two girls.

"Hey, what's up," W said. He wanted to begin some sort of fraternization. It could lead to a score. "You got a light?" he asked. He spoke to the taller of the two boys. Bush pulled his pack of mangled Camels from his pocket. He withdrew a mashed cigarette. He offered the boy one. The boy said he was all set. Bush straightened out the cigarette. He placed it between his lips. He leaned over toward the boy he had asked for a light. The boy pulled a shiny stainless Zippo lighter from his pocket. He flipped the top. He flipped the flint wheel with his thumb. He lighted W's Camel.

"Hey thanks boss," Bush told the boy. He took a drag on his cigarette. "Hey, you guys been inside?" Bush asked him.

"Yeah, just came out," the boy said. "Any chance you could make us a buy?" Bush asked.

"Uh, yeah, I guess so," the boy replied.

"We'll give ya a couple bucks extra," Bush told him.

"Cool," the boy said.

Bush pulled a wad of bills from his rear pocket. He handed the boy two $5 bills. "Couple six-packs. Whatever they've got. Doesn't matter much," Bush said.

"OK," the boy said. "Stand by."

Bush held his Camel between his forefinger and thumb. He sucked a drag on his Camel. He then held the butt over McKenzie's head. He flicked the ashes. "You asshole," McKenzie said. He jumped away. He was laughing. "Horneyboy, suck on this," W replied. He put his hand between his legs. He stuck out his thumb. The others in the group waited while their friend bought booze for W. and McKenzie. They looked at Bush skeptically. They took him for really what he was. He was a wise-ass Andover preppie. His primary mission was having fun.

The boy who went inside the Beverage Mart for Bush's beer came through the door. He returned to the parking lot. The group was huddled awaiting his return. He was carrying a brown grocery bag. Inside were two six-packs of Knickerbockers. He handed off the bag to Bush. He reached into his pocket for the change. He handed Bush $6.55. Bush took a buck sixty-five. He handed the $5 bill to his supplier.

"Hey man thanks!" the boy said.

"Busman, you earned it," Bush told his supplier. "Catch you guys later." W and McKenzie walked across the parking lot. They headed for the bus stop.

Snap! McKenzie was walking behind Bush. He heard the noise. He suspected what W was up to. Bush had pulled the tab on one of the cold Knickerbockers. "Horneyboy, want one?" W asked McKenzie. Bush had helped himself.

"Man that's sweet. Sweet, baby." He took another swig. He swallowed loudly. He exaggerated the pleasure. He shared it with his audience. McKenzie was laughing.

"Yeah, gimme one of those, Bushie," he told his friend. Bush pulled a can from the bag. He handed it to McKenzie. McKenzie pulled the tab. He was about to take a swig. Bush held up his can. He clicked McKenzie's. He said, "Cheers, Horneyboy."

The two boys continued to enjoy their cold beers. They waited for the bus. It would bring them back to campus. The uptown bus arrived. Bush jumped in first. McKenzie followed. They dropped their fares into the cashbox. They took two seats near the back of the bus. There, they continued to enjoy their beers. They were out of the driver's immediate eyesight. They neared the end of the brief 2.3-mile ride back to Andover. McKenzie stood up. He pulled the stop cord. The driver pulled over two blocks ahead. He opened the doors. Bush and McKenzie exited from the door toward the rear. They began walking up the hill. They headed to their dorm.

They got close to the dorm. Bush told McKenzie, "Keep cool. I see Hart." He was referring to John Hart. Hart, the headmaster, was walking on the green. The boys headed to their dorm. "Afternoon, Mr. Headmaster," W exclaimed. He addressed Hart. It wasn't easy hiding the huge brown grocery bag. The bag hid the six-packs. There was no option at this point.

"Good afternoon, fellas," Hart said jauntily. He passed them. Hart had that air about him. It suggested he knew the boys should be in class. Yet he didn't press the boys on what they were up to. The boys passed him. Bush mumbled under his breath to McKenzie. "Holy shit, that was too close for comfort." Reason to celebrate. Passing by the headmaster with two six-packs of beer in the middle of the school day was an achievement. They hadn't gotten caught. Bush pulled out from the bag the beer he had been swigging. He took a swig. He swallowed loudly. "Heaven," he said to his buddy. "Pure heaven, Horneyboy."

When they got to the dorm, the boys entered a side door. They went to the second floor. Bush's room was on the second floor. Bush pulled out a key. He opened the door. The boys entered the room. Bush began stashing the beer in a small dorm refrigerator. The 'frig contained nothing beyond a bottle of water and a can of Cott ginger ale. Bush kicked off his loafers. He threw on a pair of cowboy boots. His father had bought them for him in Houston. The gift was in honor of his going away to prep school in New England. In New England nobody except freaks of nature wears cowboy boots. He then thumbed through his record collection. He pulled out a Beatles Favorite Hits album. He placed a record on his Marantz turntable. He placed the needle at the beginning of "Let It Be." He pulled another beer from the refrigerator. He popped the tab. He lay back in an overstuffed easy chair he had found at the bottom of someone's driveway on trash day. He relaxed.

"Horney, lock the door," Bush instructed McKenzie. McKenzie jumped up. He pushed the button on the door to Bush's bedroom. McKenzie then sat on the edge of Bush's bunk bed. He began sipping a Knickerbocker. "What are they serving tonight at mess?" Bush asked McKenzie.

"Dunno," McKenzie said. "Oh, it's Friday night. That means steaks. Cool."

The boys continued to drink. They listened to the Beatles. Bush heard the pay phone in the hallway ringing. Typically he ignored it. He would let someone else answer it. Usually it was a bogus call from a marketing company. A few moments later, someone was knocking on Bush's bedroom door. "Who is it?" Bush asked. He was worried. It might be the resident advisor.

"Phone's for you W," said the voice on the other side.

"It's your mom," the voice said.

"Shit, OK," Bush yelled. "Thanks." He took a swig of beer. He put the unfinished can in the refrigerator. He opened the door to get the phone. He closed the door behind him. Again, he told McKenzie to lock it. "Hello?" Bush said in to the phone.

"Georgie. It's your mother."

"Hey Mummsy!" he replied. "What's up?"

"Just wanted to say hi and see how you are, honey," she said. "How is school going?"

"OK Mummsy - for school," he said.

She was expecting something of the kind.

"Honey, I hope you're studying hard and getting good grades," she replied.

"Y-y-y-yeah, Mummsy," he replied.

"George?" she asked.

"Mummsy, I'm doin' OK. Honest," he told her.

"OK Georgie," she said. "Be a good boy." She said nothing to him about the letter she had received from the headmaster's office. The letter about her son's misbehaving in home room recently. It was the time when he had hit the home-room teacher with a paper clip. He had fired the paper clip from a rubber band. "You sound tired," she said. "Are you OK?"

"Yeah, Mummsy, just tired of studying," he told her.

"Well, OK," she said. "Take care of yourself. Just a second, your father wants to say hi."

"Hi young man," George H.W. Bush said. "You working hard?"

"No," W answered. "Hardly working."

"Son, you be good. Study hard and make your grampa proud, and me too," his father said. "You'll be home for Thanksgiving. We'll see you then."

"OK, Daddio," W replied. "Au revoir, Pop."

"Bye, son," his father said. He was tentative. He hung up the phone.

Georgie sounded tired to his mother. It was not surprising. He was in the middle of another drinking binge. He had consumed already more than 16 ounces of beer. It was only 24 hours after he had drunk himself sick.

"Did you ask him anything about the letter?" Barbara Bush asked her husband? They hung up the phone back in Houston. They had just had a brief chat with their eldest child.

"Um, no, uh, no," George H.W. Bush replied. "We can't watch him 24 hours a day Bar."

She was worried, however, about her son. "He sounded tired to me," she told her husband. "I don't know what's going on but I hope he's doing OK." Barbara Bush was in motherly denial. But what could she do?

After hanging up the phone, W headed back to his room. He lost his balance momentarily. He turned and tried to open the door. It was locked. He had asked McKenzie to lock it. But W had been drinking. His perceptions were becoming a little cloudy. He realized, however, now that the door was locked. He had asked McKenzie to lock it. He knocked on the door. "Horneyboy, open up," he yelled.

"Coming," McKenzie yelled.

"That's what she said," W replied.

McKenzie opened the door. Bush entered. He walked over to the refrigerator. He wanted to grab the unfinished beer he had put there when he went to take his mother's call. He picked up the can. He took a big mouthful of cold beer. He swallowed loudly. "Man o' man, that's good stuff," he said. He finished off the can. He squeezed it tightly in his hand. He tossed it across the room toward a small dorm-sized metal waste basket. The can hit the basket. It made a big bang.

"Two points!" Bushie shouted. He reached back into the refrigerator for another Knickerbocker. Snap. He popped the tab. He held the can up in the air. "Here's to you, Horneyboy," he said. "Hope we get laid soon."

W jumped onto his upper bunk. He laid down to relax.

"Time to start thinking about dinner, eh Horneyboy?" Bush said.

"Yeah, W," McKenzie said. "Let's finish these beers. Then maybe we can head over."

Friday nights was a good time to go to the dining hall in Bradford Hall. Bradford Hall was a women's dorm. But on Fridays and Saturdays its dining room was co-ed. Such was the case in the school's other dining rooms on Fridays and

Saturdays. Bush drank his beer quickly. He launched the empty can. He tossed it toward the waste basket. "Yes!" he yelled. "Two more points. Horneyboy, let's book."

McKenzie wasn't as fast a drinker as Bushie. "Hold on," he said. "I've got a few more swallows."

"Swallow this," Bush replied. He jumped off the bed. "Let's truck asshole," Bush said. "We've also got to get more beer."

McKenzie rushed to finish his beer. He tossed his empty can into the basket. The boys headed out the door. "Wait, hold on," W said suddenly. "I don't wanna leave those empties there. If the RA comes around he may smell the odor." He turned around. He let himself back into his room. He saw the empty brown grocery bag on his desk. He figured he could use it for trashing the empties somewhere. He took the bag over to the waste basket. He dumped the empties into the bag. "Let's go," W said to McKenzie. They left the room. Now Bush had to get rid of the empties. But they still had some remnants of beer in them. The bag started dripping as the boys walked down the stairs. They were headed to the first floor. "Great," Bush said. "Just what I need." When they got to the first floor, Bush saw a trash barrel just outside the front door. He and McKenzie went out the door. Bush tossed the bag into the barrel. The boys began walking to Bradford Hall.

"Mr. Bush?" said a voice behind them. Bush turned around. He recognized the voice. It was Jim Thorpe, the resident advisor. Thorpe has been coming out of his quarters. He was also on the way to dinner. He smelled the beer. He followed the trail of spills. He assumed it might have come from Bush's room. He fetched the bag from the barrel. He found the empties. "These yours?"

"Uh, no," Bush said.

"No?" asked Thorpe. Bush looked at McKenzie. McKenzie didn't know what to say. Or do.

"George, look, you know alcohol is prohibited here, especially if you're underage," Thorpe instructed. "If these are yours, then make them your last." Bush didn't acknowledge they were his. McKenzie also refused to take credit for their ownership.

"10-4," Bush told Thorpe. "Gotchyah."

Thorpe assumed the cans were Bush's, or McKenzie's, or whoever's. But he wasn't prepared at this time of the day to make an issue out of it. If it happened again, then he'd take some sort of action.

W and McKenzie continued on to Bradford Hall. They walked up to the front door. They took a left to get to the dining hall. They walked up to the food line. Each pulled an orange plastic food tray from the pile. The pile of trays was located at the beginning of the line. They made their way down the line. They chose the specialty of Friday nights. It was steak and fries. The choice of vegetable was green peas or broccoli. McKenzie asked the dining-room attendant for the broccoli. Junior had ghastly memories of broccoli. He suddenly remembered the day when he was just five years old. His mother had made broccoli for dinner. She'd also made spare ribs and baked potatoes. Spare ribs and potatoes were heaven. Broccoli was hell. The family had been living in Midland, Texas. It was 1950. "Gag me," Junior said as he saw the broccoli. "Gross."

"Spare me the details," McKenzie said to W.

"Horneyboy, the stuff is disgusting," Bush replied. He made no apologies for his commentary on McKenzie's choice. The boys paid for their meals with their meal cards at the end of the line. They proceeded to one of the long wooden tables in the dining hall. Bush sat down at a table occupied by two other boys. A girl was also at the table. Bush recognized her. She was in his math class. Her name was Sharon Taft. Sharon had red hair and freckles. Bush, of course, had given her a nickname. The nickname played off her looks and her surname.

"Hey Freckiegirl," he said. He was smiling. Taft was self-conscious about her freckles. She tried to hide her disdain. But W was well-known as a wisecracker.

He sat down. She quickly smelled something. She perceived it to be beer.

"W," she said. "How's the beer?"

"Be better if I had some here," Bush replied. "Horneyboy, let's chow so we can get back to our refreshments."

Bush and McKenzie finished their meals. They got ready to leave. McKenzie stood up with his tray and dirty dishes. He walked over to the area where students were supposed to leave the trays and dishes. Bush left his on the table.

"W," Taft said. She was proud she was able to call the Bushman on something. "Forget something?"

"Yeah, Freckiegirl" he shot back. "Condoms."

She shook her head. She rolled her eyes. "That's good, W. Real impressive."

"Thanks F-girl," he said. He tried a variation on a theme. "Later, chickie."

With McKenzie in tow, Bush left the dining room. He headed back to the dorm. He had one priority. He wanted to get back to the room to resume his latest beer fest. On the way out he stopped by a vending machine. He wanted some munchies. Chitos would do the trick. Or, She-toes, as he called them. He dropped some change into the machine. He pulled the lever for She-toes. Bush and his buddy were on their way to another party. They walked to the dorm. Bush pulled the bag of She-toes open. He grabbed a couple with his fingers. He tossed one up in the air. He tipped his head. He opened his mouth wide. He missed the She-toe. He lost his balance. His left shoulder struck McKenzie squarely in the chest.

"Jesus Christ," McKenzie yelled. "Can you slow down?"

"Damn, Horney" W replied. "One good She-toe on the ground." He tossed up another. This time he caught it. "Two points!" he yelled. "How 'bout that, Horney?"

"Great asshole, very impressive," McKenzie said.

The two boys walked up to the dorm. They went in the front door. They headed up to Bush's room. Bush jammed the bag of She-toes in his mouth. He reached in his pocket for his room key. He stuck his key in the door. He made a dash for the refrigerator. He grabbed a cold can of Knickerbocker. "Join me Horney?"

"Yeah," McKenzie said.

He grabbed a second can. He tossed it behind his back to McKenzie. McKenzie was taken by surprise. He missed the can. It hit the concrete-block wall. It burst open. Beer and foam sprayed all over the place. "Horney, you just ruined a good beer," he said. He was laughing. "Want another one?"

McKenzie shook his head in amazement. He said, "No, thanks. I'll get my own." Snap.

Bush pulled the tab on his beer. He hopped on to the bunk bed. He took a big gulp. He swallowed loudly. "Here's to America Horney," he said.

Chapter IV
Endless Slummer

George W. Bush finished his senior year in 1964 at Phillips Andover. A week later he had an older friend from Kennebunkport sign for him to rent a U-Haul truck. The truck lot was on the outskirts of Andover. He drove the truck over to his dorm. He haphazardly threw all his stuff into the back for the trip to Maine. Each summer the Bush family would meet at the Bush compound in late May. He had decided to skip commencement ceremonies. He felt they would be a boring afterthought. He believed they would be too rigidly structured for his liking. He had told John Hart, the headmaster at Andover, to send his diploma in the mail. Hart wasn't surprised. He had come to know George W. Bush. W was a precocious kid. He hid well his brilliance. Hart didn't know whether it was intentional or not.

This would be his last summer in Maine. It would soon be time to start the real work. He would be attending Yale University. That would occur the following September. The school was located in W's hometown of New Haven, Conn. It was also where his father had captained the baseball team. He'd be expected to follow in his father's footsteps. He would be expected to be his father's academic and athletic legacy.

If W needed an excuse to drink while at Andover, summers required fewer excuses. Bush needed something cold to drink. He wouldn't be needing justification to pursue it this summer. He had plans once he got back to Maine. He would meet friends at Allison's. It was a restaurant and bar in downtown Kennebunkport. It had become a landmark nightspot for the younger set. Many adults also liked the place.

The drive from Andover to Kennebunkport took almost 2 ½ hours. W arrived at the family's summer homestead on Ocean Avenue. He pulled up into the winding driveway. The sky was clear blue. The sun was shining brightly. It was a heavenly spring day on the southern coast of Maine. Seagulls were prancing about at the ocean's edge. They were looking for scraps of seafood. A few lobster boats bobbed in the bay just outside the Bush's home. W jumped out of the truck. He slammed the heavy door. He walked up to the big cottage. "Mummsy?" he called out.

Mummsy, as it turned out, was still back in Texas. She was with senior. He was in the final stages of a grueling U.S. Senate campaign against Ralph Yarborough. A maid and a cleaning crew were helping open up the cottages that summer. It would give George and Barbara Bush whatever extra moments they had to campaign.

"Junior, that you?" yelled Ethel Watkins. She was the maid who the Bush family had employed for years.

"It's señor to you," W replied sarcastically. He was getting old enough to resent the Junior moniker. It made him feel he was being belittled as a castoff of his father. He shared his pop's first name. Señor was also W's crafty variation on "senior." That was the informal way people referred to George H.W. Bush in differentiating the two in conversation.

"OK, George," Watkins replied. She came to the front door from the living room. She had been dusting. She gave W a big hug. She loved his contrariness.

"Welcome home from school," she said. "Imagine, you're all through!"

"EW," Junior said. "You got any beer? Man, it's been a long drive."

"Junior, uh, Georgie, what are you talking about - beer?" Watkins asked.

"EW, it's between us, just like always, OK?" W replied. He was smiling.

"Oh Georgie, you charmer you," she replied. EW had known George W. Bush since he was a baby. To her, he was like one of her own children. Watkins was single and had no children of her own. She really thought of George W. as a son, her son. But at the same time, she was more like an aunt to him. Or maybe even a grandmother. He loved her in that way. Yet there were no strings attached. Watkins never disciplined George W. She never threatened him in a way a parent might a child who was misbehaving or even thinking of misbehaving.

W walked from near the front of the house to the kitchen. He headed to the refrigerator. He opened the heavy white steel door on the refrigerator. He glanced up and down the shelves. He was looking for anything to drink or eat. Then he looked on the inside of the refrigerator door. He saw on the second shelf two bottles of Grolsch. It was an expensive German beer that was sold in fancy brown bottles. They had ceramic tops that had rubber gaskets and metal flips. "Hmmm," he said. Watkins shadowed him. She was interested in seeing W and chatting with him after a long absence. She hadn't seen him since the previous summer. She wasn't thinking about his looking for beer in the refrigerator. "What you got George?" Watkins asked W.

"Well, EW," he replied, "I see some of pop's Grolsch here. Pop's, I assume."

"Yeah, and I think that's just where it should stay," she told Junior. He hadn't said anything about drinking it. Not yet anyway. But Watkins sensed that that was the next plan.

"EW, anyone else's this could be?" W asked Watkins. It was like he was ready to drink it if it were his father's. Yet if it were someone else's he would be more hesitant to take it. W had a distant relationship with his father. It was slightly different from the relationship between him and his mother.

"Junior - sorry, George, I assume it's your father's. But it really doesn't matter," Watkins told him. She was wiping the beige Formica counter with a damp, plaid-fabric dish rag. "Just leave it there. Get your stuff out of the truck."

"OK," he said. He closed the refrigerator door. He headed outside to start unpacking the U-Haul. He opened the rear doors of the truck. He grabbed a couple of brown grocery bags. They contained some of his dirty laundry from school. He returned to the house. He went into the basement. The clothes washer and dryer were located there.

"Hey EW," he yelled up the cellar stairs.

"Yes George?" Watkins replied from the study. She was dusting George H.W. Bush's library collection.

"OK if I leave this stuff next to the hamper down here?" W asked.

"What stuff honey?" Watkins asked him.

"You know, my laundry," he replied.

Watkins laughed. "Yeah, how soon I forget," she laughed. "I'll take care of it sweetie, Watkins told her "surrogate son."

W left his dirty laundry next to the washer. He ran up the stairs. He was skipping every other step. He was back in the kitchen. He opened the refrigerator door. He grabbed one of the Grolsch beers. The bottle was nice and cold. Bush was perspiring. He was thirsty. He opened the bottle. He tried to muffle the sound by holding it under his cloth-and-flannel Andover letter jacket. He hoped this would prevent Watkins from hearing what he was up to. On the other hand, he could have taken the bottle outside to open it. She would clearly have heard nothing. So it was only a half-hearted attempt to keep from her what he was up to. He didn't really care either way. Whether she knew or not didn't really matter to him. He sort of wanted her to know. If she didn't, that would be OK, too.

"George," he heard Watkins say. "What are you up to?"

"Nothing EW," he replied.

"George, didn't I hear something?"

"Dunno, EW," he said. He was toying with her. "What do you think you heard?"

"OK, dear, just behave yourself," she said. She didn't press the issue any further.

"Cool, EW," he said. He usually used her initials, in lieu of her name. That was George W. Bush's way of keeping a distance from close affection. He would control the extent of the relationship. It was the magic of his practice of assigning nicknames to anyone he could.

Bush took a big gulp of the cold Grolsch. He swallowed loudly, of course. He walked from the kitchen. He went out the front door. He headed to the truck. "Ahhh," he said. He expressed it within earshot of anyone who would care to hear. In this case, no one heard. But George W. Bush made his point nonetheless. He grabbed another handful of stuff from the truck. It included his hi-fi and its myriad components. He dragged them back to the house. All the while, he kept close watch on his beverage of choice. He made several trips to and from the truck. He kept himself well lubricated in the process. W took the last sip of the Grolsch. He brought the empty bottle to a tiny stainless sink. The sink was in the utility room. The room was at the back entrance to the house. He turned on the cold water spigot. He began rinsing out the bottle. These Grolsch bottles were collectibles to many Grolsch fanciers. W remembered two of them. They were on a shelf in his father's study in Houston. So, like father, like son. After rinsing out the empty he walked to his room. His room was on the back side of the house. It overlooked the open ocean.

He proudly placed it on top of a pine bookcase. The bookshelf was next to the window overlooking the water.

Bush then went to the kitchen again. He opened the door to the refrigerator. He pulled out the remaining bottle of Grolsch beer. He closed the refrigerator door.

"George, if you're hungry I made mixed up some fresh salmon and mayonnaise this morning," Watkins yelled from the den. "It's delicious if you wanna make a sandwich. There's some fresh rye bread from Bradbury's in the bread drawer." Bradbury's Market in nearby Cape Porpoise was a favorite grocery store. Many of the locals shopped there regularly. The market also did a land-sale business to tourists. They would flock there in droves during the summer. Bradbury's carried bread that the Bradbury family baked daily.

"Jeez, that doesn't sound bad if I say so myself," W replied to Watkins. "Hey, EW, does that include a side of chips?"

Junior figured he'd get in a wisecrack. He had transformed Watkins into his waitress. That cold Grolsch beer that he had just finished put a nice edge on things. So he was feeling especially cocky.

"For you, yes," Watkins yelled to him. "There should also be a bag o' chips in the bread drawer. And help yourself to milk or whatever."

Her idea of "whatever" didn't include beer. It also didn't include any other type of beverage if it contained alcohol. She innocently offered her surrogate son something cold and nutritious to drink with his lunch.

W told her, "EW, I guess I'll make myself a sandwich."

"OK, good," she said. "You need to put some flesh on those bones." W was all skin and bones. Chip off the old block. His father was built the same way. He had virtually no fat on him. He picked up that enviable trait from his father. His mother had a tendency to put on weight. She'd had six kids and one miscarriage. His sister Dorothy was also prone to weight.

The top of the second Grolsch was off with a snap. Young George was about to enjoy himself some more. It was great being home for the summer. Kennebunkport, Maine, was a great place to enjoy the summer. The Bush family was among the wealthiest in town. It had one of the priciest pieces of real estate to claim as its own.

"M-m-m-m-m good," W said. The beer made summer in Kennebunkport all the smoother.

"That salmon good?" Watkins yelled to him.

"Uh, yeah, really good," W replied. He hadn't even opened the bowl of salmon. He hadn't even fetched from the refrigerator. The "m-m-m-m-m good" that Watkins heard him mutter was the smooth taste of that second, cold Grolsch beer. He quickly pulled the bowl of salmon from the refrigerator. He placed it on the counter. The counter was next to the kitchen sink. He removed the cellophane from the top of the bowl. He grabbed a stainless-steel fork from the middle-cabinet drawer. He opened the bread drawer. It was just below the silverware drawer. He removed the plastic bag containing a sliced loaf of Bradbury's rye bread. It had just been baked the hours before. He removed two slices. He put them on the counter. He began slathering them with the salmon mix. Next to the sandwich he was making, W had placed the bottle of Grolsch. He paused and picked it up. He took a huge gulp. "Wow, that's good," he said. No one was around to hear the exclamation. If Watkins had heard him, all the better. Living dangerously. It was fun.

"Glad you like it," he heard her say. He put down the beer. He sliced the sandwich. He pulled a sharp knife from the drawer. The drawer was to the left of the silverware drawer. He removed a wooden-handled knife. It had a serrated blade. He cut the sandwich in half. He removed a white porcelain plate from the cupboard. It was above the counter. He put the sandwich on the plate. He grabbed the plate. He grabbed also his Grolsch. He walked over to the table.

"George, you really shouldn't be drinking beer," Watkins said. She had walked into the kitchen and saw what he was up to.

"Why, whose is it?" he asked her. He half-pretended he thought she was concerned because he was drinking from his father's favorite stash.

"George, honey, it doesn't matter whose it is," she said. "You are too young to be drinking beer."

"How about gin?" he asked. He laughed. He took another big gulp of Grolsch. It would help wash down a mouthful of his sandwich. She shook her head. She closed her eyes. This was no one to tangle with. This was W.

W finished his sandwich - and beer. He figured he needed a rest. He went into his bedroom. He jumped up on the bed. He lay on his back. He grabbed a deck of cards. They were in his nightstand. He began shuffling them. He was feeling pretty good. He was getting drunk. He picked up the phone next to his bed. He dialed Missy Philbrick. He hoped she was home from school for the summer.

"Hello?" said a voice on the other end of the phone.

"Hey, Miss-fit!" he said. He was excited.

"W! What's up? When d'you get home?"

"Little while ago," he said. "Whatcha doin'? Wanna go downtown?"

"Yeah, what the heck," she said. "Wanna check out Allison's?" She figured it would be fun to stop by the popular restaurant. It also had a bar. Lots of kids used to hang around there. They'd hang around inside. They'd hang around outside.

"Yeah, I'll be over in 'bout half an hour or so," W replied.

"OK," Philbrick said. "See ya then."

W wasn't sure now what he would use for a vehicle. He knew he could probably get away with persuading Watkins to let him use her VW Beetle. But then again it would be more of a gas to use the old red Jeep. The Jeep had a ragtop. It would be fun to run downtown with. Bush then realized the Jeep's registration might be expired. If it were even registered at all. He jumped up. He walked outside. The Jeep was parked on the front side of the house. That was the side visible from Ocean Avenue. He walked up to the Jeep. He wanted to check it out. It had a Maine plate on the rear. He didn't bother checking to see if it had one on the front. Maine law required two plates. A plate was good enough for W. The ragtop was up. But it was a mess. The plastic windows were old and yellowed. They were virtually impossible to see through. There was a gash in the rear window. The Jeep was rarely used. It was usually used only during the summers. Otherwise it basically sat outside the Bush house. George H.W. Bush used it to run around the property. Rarely did the Jeep go off the compound.

W decided to fold down the top. It was a sunny day. It was fairly mild. Having the top down would be fun. W also figured Philbrick would enjoy it. As the saying goes, school's out. Time to celebrate the season. W jumped in the driver's seat. He unbolted the roof's windshield hooks. It freed up the top. He pushed it back. He folded it in the rear of the Jeep. He then removed the two side doors. He threw them in the back. The floor had an inch of water in it. Such was life in W's Jeep.

"Hey EW," he yelled as he ran into the house. "I'll catchyah later."

"What's up George?" she asked.

"Gonna run over to Miss-fit's," he replied. "We're gonna run down to Allison's."

"Missy home from school?" Watkins asked W.

"Obviously, or I wouldn't be going over," the wisecracker replied.

"George W. Bush, what am I going to do with you?" Watkins asked. "OK honey, be careful. Wait - how are you getting down there?"

"The Jeep," he replied.

"Uh, are you sure? I, um, I don't think. George, I'm really not sure you should use the Jeep," she said. She knew of its frail condition. She also knew that young George Bush had just drunk two beers. Two she knew of, anyway.

"It'll be OK," he said. "No prob. Maybe see ya tomorrow."

"OK, George. Be careful. Say hi to Missy for me," she said to him.

"Miss-fit," he corrected her.

"OK, George, Miss-fit," Watkins said. She picked up on the nickname he'd given Philbrick.

He laughed approvingly. He went outside. He hopped in the Jeep. He turned the ever-present key to the "on" position. He pushed the starter button. After several turnovers Bush let off the starter button. He paused a couple of seconds. Again he pushed the starter button. With a few sputters and coughs the old Jeep finally came to life. Puffs of black smoke came from its tailpipe. Watkins happened to look out the front window. She saw all the black smoke.

"Lord Mercy," she said. She muttered quietly to herself. She wondered what W was up to now. "There's no stopping that boy," she whispered.

W pushed in the clutch. He moved the shift stick into first gear. He let out the clutch. He was on his way to Philbrick's house. It was just a few blocks away. It was just off Ocean Avenue. He pulled out from the Bush's long meandering driveway. He took a left onto Ocean Avenue. Less than a half-mile later, Bush pulled into a gravel driveway. He drove up to the Philbrick's house. It was a large weathered-shingle cape.

It had a big white, brick chimney running up the side be-tween the house and a screened-in porch.

Bush shut down the noisy, smoky Jeep. He jumped out of the driver's seat. Philbrick came running from the porch. She was wearing a Wellesley sweatshirt. She'd just finished a year at the ivy-league school. She was a year older than W. She had always been one of his secret admirers. She thought he was interesting. She thought he was funny. She considered him a wisecrack. She thought he was self-conscious about his family's wealth and prominence. The Philbricks had money, too. They could afford to live on Maine's gold coast. But their wealth didn't come close to the family that built the Bush compound. Walker's Point was named for George H.W. Bush's uncle's family. It was also his mother Dorothy Walker Bush's family.

"W!" Philbrick yelled. She ran toward the Jeep.

"Miss-fit," he yelled. She gave Junior a big bear hug. He returned the gesture in kind. They pulled apart. She looked at him.

"Got any more?" she asked.

"Any more what?" he asked.

"Beer, G-man," she said. "Like you didn't know what I meant."

"Oh, wish I did," he replied. "Why, do I smell like beer?"

"Course," she said. "Let's book to Allison's. Maybe someone can buy for us."

The two hopped in the Jeep. W fired up the old beast. A cloud of smoke erupted from the vehicle. W backed out of the Philbrick's driveway. He headed downtown to Dock Square. It was the center of town. Allison's was one of the best-known landmarks. Bush was driving fast. The speed limit was 35 mph. He was going 46 mph. They rounded a sharp curve. The Jeep almost rolled over.

"Jesus Christ W," Philbrick said. She held on to the grab bar in front of her seat. Her hair was flying in the wind. "What the hell are you trying to do? You trying to kill us?"

W was too intent on maintaining control of the vehicle. He didn't respond. He was having a blast. He successfully nego-tiated the dangerous curve. He was on a roll. He was a block from Dock Square. He happened to look in the mirror. The mirror was on the outside of the driver's side of the Jeep. He saw a cop car. It was directly behind him. He tried to slow down. It was too late. He looked in the mirror again. The blue lights were on. W considered running. He realized there was nowhere to hide. He started pulling to the side of the road. He was going to stop for the police officer.

"They got me," W said to Philbrick. She hadn't realized they were being tailed by a police car.

"Great George," she said. "And you've been drinking, too. Asshole."

"Chill out," he told her. "Hope this goes quick. I'm thirsty." His place was not to worry about getting arrested. He figured he'd charm his way out of this jam.

The charmer. George W. Bush was a charmer. He had a way. Oh, did he have a way. People envied his ease. For a first-born kid, he was an odd-lot out of a class of over-achievers.

The police officer appeared at his door. He had seen the officer's stripes. He quickly figured out his rank. "Hey Sarge," Bush said gleefully.

"George, do you know why I stopped you?" Sgt. John Prescott asked Bush. Prescott knew the Bush family. This was a small town. Moreover, the Bushes were among its most prominent citizens. George H.W. Bush was a big financial contributor to many local causes. Two years ago the elder Bush had gotten to know Prescott. The department was campaigning in a bid to raise money for a new police station.

"Um, yeah, I guess I was going a little fast," W replied. He smiled. "I'm trying to get to Allison's in time for happy hour."

Prescott was taken by Junior's response. He didn't have a fast comeback. He paused. He pursed his lips. He asked to see Junior's license. Bush reached into the right rear pocket of his chinos. He pulled out a crumpled mess. He unfolded it. It revealed a tattered license. He handed to Prescott.

"Just a moment," Prescott said to him. "I need to run this." Prescott returned to his cruiser. He radioed the police dispatcher. "Bush, George W.," Prescott said into his two-way radio mike. "DOB 7/6/46." After 25 seconds, the dispatcher replied. The dispatcher was George Pescosolido. He told Prescott over the radio, "Class C, active. Two convictions, no restrictions." The record showed that George W. Bush had twice been convicted of speeding. Once was in Kennebunk, Maine, in 1962. Once was in Hillsboro, New Hampshire, in 1963. Prescott also ran the license plate on the Jeep. It came back to Barbara P. Bush. The Maine Secretary of State's Office records showed the plates with a June 30, 1963 expiration date. Prescott returned to the Jeep's driver-side door. He walked around the front of the vehicle to see if it had a plate on the front.

"Mr. Bush," he said. "I am issuing you a warning on your speed. You need to slow down. You don't need any more points on your license. I'm gonna give you a break this time." However, he issued Bush a $60 ticket for the expired plates. The ticket also was for having only one plate. The law required two. "Your mother needs to renew her registration if you're gonna drive this vehicle," Prescott said. He told Bush the Jeep would have to be towed back to the house. He called a wrecker. He offered to give Bush and Philbrick rides back to their houses.

A wrecker from Arundel Auto showed up. Bush wrote the driver a check. He asked him to tow the Jeep back to his parents' house.

"Whadda ya wanna do?" W asked Philbrick.

"I dunno," she replied. "Let's hoof it to Allison's."

"Great," W replied.

"We can always hitch a ride back," she said. "Let's head out."

"Mr. Bush," Prescott said as he was leaving the scene. "You've got to be careful." Prescott thought he'd smelled alcohol on Bush's breath. He said nothing. The way he figured it, this was Bush's lucky day. Prescott decided if he caught W in a motor-vehicle violation, there would be no more second chances.

"OK Sarge," Bush said. "Catch ya later."

"Say hi to your parents for me," Prescott said.

"Yeah, OK," Bush replied. "I'm sure they'll be real happy to hear from you." He was kidding. If he brought Prescott's regards to his parents, they would quickly surmise that he'd had some sort of run-in with the police. W and Philbrick began walking the few blocks to Dock Square. Bush was expecting he could find someone to help him score some alcohol. He was thirsty. He needed to feed his growing habit. There was a parking lot behind Allison's. Kids often congregated out there to smoke. Bush headed out there with Philbrick.

"Let's see if anyone is out here," he said to Philbrick. "Nah, on second thought, let's just go inside and see if we can order." They walked around to the front of Allison's. They walked in. They turned right. They headed for the area where the bar is surrounded by a dozen small wooden tables. Bush noticed two empty stools at the bar. He and Philbrick sat down.

"What's it gonna be, folks," asked the bartender. The bartender was known by all as Fish. Fish began wiping the bar in front of Bush and Philbrick. They were deciding what to order.

"What's on draft?" Bush asked.

"Let's see, we've got Beck's," Fish said.

"OK, sounds good," W replied.

"One Becks," Fish repeated. "And you, Miss?" he asked Philbrick.

"No, it's Missfit," Bush corrected Fish. He was laughing.

Philbrick blushed. She said nothing.

"I guess I'll have a Beck's too," she told Fish. Fish turned to pull two beer glasses. Bush and Philbrick looked at each other. They said nothing. Looks are everything. Translation: They lucked out. Fish didn't card them. As far as Fish was concerned, he'll sell a few more drinks. Better yet, he'll make more tip money, God-willing. So who needs to ask for proof of age? Fish poured the two Becks. He grabbed two napkins. He placed on the shiny wooden bar in front of his two newest customers. He placed the beers in front of them. "Enjoy," he said.

Bush needed the last word. "Don't worry," he said. "We will."

Fish had heard it all before. He smiled. Anything to preserve a tip.

"Man-o-man that tastes some good," Bush said to Philbrick. He took another big gulp.

"So W, what are you up to this summer?" she asked him.

"Oh, about 5-9," Bush replied.

"Thanks, Bush," Philbrick replied.

"Don't mention it Miss-fit," he said. "Hey, Fishboy, can I get another one?" He yelled across the bar to the bar tender.

"'Nother one?" came the reply from the bar tender. "How 'about you miss - you all set?"

"It's Missfit," W corrected him.

"I'm all set, thanks," Philbrick replied. She ignored Bush. Bush started on his second Becks. "Hey Miss-fit, what say we take out the boat?" W asked her.

"Uh, little cold out there, W," she replied.

"So what," he said. "We'll take the Whaler out for a quick spin. It'll be a gas."

Philbrick didn't reply. Bush finished his second beer. Philbrick had all-but-finished hers. He started getting up off his bar stool. "Be right back," he said. "Gotta take a whiz." She rolled her eyes.

A few minutes later, W re-appeared. "Ready for a boat ride?" he asked. She got up. W put two $5 bills on the bar. They began walking out the door. "See ya Fishboy," he shouted to the bar tender.

"Later, folks," Fish replied. "Thank you." W and Philbrick walked out the front door. Dock Square was looking quaint. Its period lanterns and small boutiques bathed in small white lights made for a quaint, small-town scene. Nearby, customers were lined up at the Clam Shack. It was located next to the drawbridge leading to Kennebunk. Summer was soon to arrive.

"Let's see if we can hitch a ride back," W said to Philbrick. They headed toward Ocean Avenue. Bush moved from the sidewalk to the edge of the narrow road. He stuck out his thumb. Several cars passed. One finally stopped. W opened the front passenger door.

"Hop in," the driver told Bush. W jumped in the front seat. Philbrick opened the right rear passenger door. She got in. "You kids headed home?" asked the driver, who recognized them both.

"Yeah, if you wooden mind," W replied. He used one of his favorite expressions. Few but himself were able to tell it from common-speak. Philbrick was accustomed to Junior's wise-cracking. But even she missed the "wooden mind" phrasing.

Bob Schultz, the driver, was headed home, too. He lived a block beyond the Bushes. His house was on the inland side of Ocean Avenue. It was in the low-rent district, so-called. He stopped just short of the Bush compound. He pulled over to the right. "This good?" he asked.

"Excellent," Bush replied. "Thanks Mr. Schlitz." The pronunciation was no mistake. This was W at his best. Or worst. He and Philbrick walked about two blocks to the driveway leading to the Bush home. They walked up the driveway. W headed to the boat shack. It was a small shed that the family used as a storage spot for fishing poles and life preservers and extra boating equipment. Also in there were gas cans, boat hooks, bumpers, extra cans of oil. W grabbed a couple of life preservers, a boat hook and a gas can.

"Come on," he said to Philbrick, "let's go for a quick ride. It was now dark. It was getting chilly. It was not the best time of day or year for boating. Only those who had to be on the water to earn a living were out. That included the local lobstermen and other fishermen along the Maine coast. Philbrick wasn't high on getting in the boat.

But she enjoyed Bush's spirit of spontaneous adventure. She followed him to the dock. That's where senior Bush usually kept the Whaler during the season. In the off-season, the boat was kept in dry-dock. The previous week the crew from Arundel Boatyard had delivered the Whaler. It had been stored for the winter at the boatyard.

"Hop in," W instructed Philbrick. He kneeled to steady the 18-foot boat with his hands. She prepared to board the boat. W pretended to push it away from the dock. He startled her. He laughed at his own humor.

"Very impressive, George," she said mockingly. She then got in the boat. She kept an eye on him the whole time. She was afraid he would pull another gag on her. He untied the mooring lines. First he unleashed bow, then the stern. He hopped in. He gave her a life preserver. She immediately put it on. He tossed his on the floor of the boa. He attached the gas can to the outboard. He stowed the hook on the right side of the boat. It was within reach of the captain's chair. He turned on the ignition. The Whaler fired up. He grabbed the hook. He pushed off the dock. He simultaneously gave the engine a bit of throttle.

W had drunk four beers in the past six hours. He'd also driven from Andover that same day. He was tired. The fatigue and the beers wasn't a good brew. He wasn't at the top of his game. But he wasn't to be slowed down. Bush cleared the dock. He gunned the engine. The Whaler's bow was now high off the choppy Atlantic Ocean. Philbrick was sitting at the stern. She was on cushioned bench seat. It extended from one side of the boat to the other. The wind was in her face. Her hair was blowing in her face.

Suddenly there was a loud thump. A bang. It happened so fast Philbrick hardly had time to react. She couldn't warn Bush to slow down. He felt the vibration. He cut the engine to a virtual stall. The sea was quiet. The stillness was broken by a loud grinding.

"Swap places with me," W told Philbrick. She moved to the front. He moved to the stern. He kneeled on the bench seat. He peered over the back of the boat. He looked toward the surface of the water. He was able to cock the engine. He could see the prop. The prop was mangled. It had hit something in the water. W had forgotten to bring the marine radio-telephone. He couldn't call for help. They were fairly close to shore. They were maybe 1,000 yards out. W decided they should try to limp their way back to the dock. He motioned to Philbrick. He wanted to swap places with her. Again he idled the engine. He grabbed an oar from the storage compartment. He tried to push the boat with the oar in the water.

"If we make it back we'll plan on celebrating tomorrow at Allison's," W told Philbrick.

Philbrick appreciated his apparent optimism. "You can go to Allison's by yourself W," she said. "I think I'll pass."

He was fighting the tide with nearly no power. It took nearly an hour for W and his passenger to get back to the dock. They neared the dock. W jumped from the bow. He had a tow line in hand to tie up. "Throw me that line," he told Philbrick. He was referring to the stern line. She tossed him the rope. He tied off the stern. She stood up. She made her way on to the dock. She was shivering. Her teeth were chattering. Her lips were blue.

"I need to go inside, fast," she told W. She headed to the house. "Come on."

"I gotta grab some stuff," W told her. "Go ahead. I'll be in in a minute." Philbrick headed in to the house. W grabbed a few things from the boat. He walked to the boat shed. He threw them inside the shed. He headed for the house.

He got just inside the front door. He kicked off his wet Quoddy boat shoes. He walked through the kitchen and living room. He got to a large bathroom. He found Philbrick grabbing a bath towel from a linen closet just outside the bathroom. She was still shivering. She was wet. "Grab a warm shower Miss-fit," he told her.

"Really?" she asked. "It's OK?"

"You're family," W replied. He leaned over. He gave her a light kiss on her left cheek. Miss-fit seemed surprised by the show of physical affection. She had rarely seen George W. Bush in such a mood.

"OK, thanks," she told him. "Now get out of here." He laughed at her humor. He grabbed another towel and snapped it at her behind. Then he left her to herself. Philbrick closed the bathroom door. She undressed in the boudoir. She left her clothes on an old wooden chair. The Bushes always kept a chair in the hallway between the bathroom and the boudoir. She turned on the hot-water faucet in the tiled, stall shower. It began heating up. She turned on the cold-water faucet. She stepped in to the shower. She luxuriated in its warmth.

W was now in his bedroom. He had thrown off his damp chinos and polo shirt. He had wrapped a big white Turkish towel around his waist. He was feeling a bit chilled too, now. The cold, ill-fated ride in his father's Whaler was over, thank God.

W also wanted to take a warm shower. He thought it might be fun to hop in the shower with Philbrick. He was about to act on that plan. The phone rang. W reached over to his nightstand. He picked up the receiver.

"Georgie?"

It was W's mother. She was calling from Texas.

"Hey Mummsy," W said into the phone. "What's up?"

"We're hoping to be up this weekend, honey," she told her eldest child. "Has Ethel finished cleaning?" Barbara Bush depended on the little people to get her summer mansion in order. Ethel Watkins was one of those people.

"Looks clean enough to me Mummsy," W replied.

"I'm not sure what that means?" his mother joked. "But I'll trust you. OK - wait, your father wants to say hi."

"Hey Junior," George H.W. Bush said in to the phone. "How's everything up in Maine. You done any fishin' yet?"

"Yeah," W replied. "Miss-fit is in the shower right now. I'm about to join her."

"No, son, I didn't mean that kind--" his father said.

"I know Pop," W interrupted his father. "But to answer your question, no."

"How's my Whaler?" senior Bush asked. "Did the boys bring it over from Arundel?"

"Yeah, it's here," W replied. "Actually, me and Miss-fit took it out for a spin a little while ago."

"Oh?" his father replied.

"Yeah, Pop," his son said. "We had a little problem."

"What happened?" the father asked.

"I dunno," W replied. "I think I hit something with the prop. We limped it back to shore."

"When did this happen?" the father asked.

"Little while ago," W replied.

"Wait. It's already 8:30 where you are," his father said. "You took it out after dark?"

"Well, uh, yeah," W replied.

"Jiminy," his father answered. He was mad. "What were you thinking?"

"I was thinking I might get laid," W replied.

"George, we'll handle this when I get up there," his father said. He hung up the phone in disgust.

W was what he was - cut from his father's cloth. His father had generally led a God-fearing life. He grew up the son of a taskmaster. But so too did George H.W. Bush see his way to getting into a few scrapes of his own. W took from his father the resentment of growing up in the presence of a set of demanding parents. For those types, nothing was good enough.

After hanging up the phone, Junior was about to head into the bathroom. He heard Philbrick turn off the shower. "Hey Miss-fit," he hollered, "I'll be right in."

She'd heard what he'd said. She pretended not to. "What's that?" she asked. By then he was opening the bathroom door. Philbrick was toweling off from the shower. She feigned surprise. "George!" she said.

"Yes, ma'am?" he replied, whipping off his towel. He was laughing. She was still wet. Her hair was dripping. He gave her a huge bear hug. He held her for several seconds. He picked up part of her towel. He began drying her hair. She enjoyed the attention. She'd always had a secret crush on this kid.

"George," she said softly.

"Yeah Miss-fit?" he asked.

She didn't reply. He began caressing her shoulders. He rubbed her back softly. She closed her eyes.

The phone started ringing. "You better get it," Philbrick told W.

"Why?" he teased.

"Because it might be your parents again," she said. "Please, W, get the phone. I don't want to get in trouble."

He kissed her on the cheek. He left to get the phone. He picked up the receiver.

"George, I want you to call the boatyard and talk to them about the damage to the Whaler," W's father instructed. "I want that boat ready for this weekend when I get up there."

"Understood," W replied. He slammed down the phone. He didn't want to hear his father say anything else.

Just about then, Philbrick yelled to him. "Jesus, George, I've gotta get home."

"Hell with that," he answered. "Tell your parents you're gonna stay here tonight."

"But they"-- she started saying.

"They have no idea my parents aren't here," he replied. "Just call 'em up. Tell 'em my parents asked you to spend the night." He walked into the den as he was talking. He knelt before the cherry liquor cabinet. He opened the glass-knobbed door. Inside was an assortment of bottles. Beefeater gin, Glenlivet scotch, Jim Beam bourbon. He reached in. He retrieved the Jim Beam. He placed it on the glass-covered top of the cabinet. He pulled a crystal snifter from the china cupboard next to the cabinet. Wrong type of vessel, but who's watching? He unscrewed the top of the Jim Beam. He poured a couple of inches into the glass.

"Here's to a good summer," he said to Philbrick. He took a good swig. He clenched his mouth. He squeezed his eye shut. It was so bitter. He swallowed hard. "Man, now that's a drink!" he said. "Hey Miss-fit, whaddayagonna have?" he asked.

"George, I need to decide what to do," she said.

"Here," he said, "this may help." He handed her the glass of Jim Beam. She looked at him quizzically.

"I dunno if I should," she said.

"Ah, go ahead," he urged.

She took a sip. She almost gagged.

"OK, call your parents," W said.

"OK," she replied. "Gimme another sip first. I need some courage." She reached for the glass. She took a larger drink this time. Again, she almost choked. By now the shock was giving her the courage to call home. She went to W's room.

She sat down on the edge of the bed. She picked up the phone. She dialed her parents. "Ma?" she said.

"Yes, darling," her mother replied. "Where are you?"

"I'm over at the Bushes. I guess I'll stay here tonight," the girl told her mother.

"Well, is it OK with the Bushes?" her mother asked. She referred to Barbara and George Bush.

"Yeah," her daughter replied.

"OK, if it's all right with them," her mother said. "We'll see you tomorrow honey. Be a good girl. Love ya."

"Love you too, Mom," Miss-fit told her mother. She then hung up the phone.

"W, we're all set," she said. "Now bring me some more of that God-awful stuff. Now, Mister."

W fetched the bottle of Jim Beam. He grabbed another glass. He poured a couple of shots in to each glass. He handed one of the glasses to Philbrick. "Cheerios Miss-Fit," he said to Philbrick. He raised his glass, He clicked it with hers.

"Cheers to you Georgie-boy," she replied. She clicked her glass with his. She was now clearly feeling the effects of the first shots she drank. That's why she was calling George W. Bush "Georgie-boy."

"And to you Georgie-girl," Bush said. "Hey, hey Georgie-girl."

The two of them were sitting on the edge of W's bed. They were drinking shots of Jim Beam. Bush leaned over to his left. He slowly put his right hand on Philbrick's right shoulder. He kissed her on the right side of her face. A second later, he kissed her slowly on the lips. Philbrick's guard was now down. She took her right hand. She held Bush's left shoulder. They continued embracing. They were kissing. They parted lips momentarily. Bush reached to the light switch by the headboard. He turned off the lamp on the nightstand. He began pulling down the covers on his bed. W began removing Philbrick's towel wrap. He removed his own. She looked at him. The two placed their glasses of Jim Beam on the nightstand. They got under the covers. The Bush house was dark. It was quiet. W opened his eyes. Sunlight was streaming in the window. He looked at his watch. It was 8:42 a.m. Philbrick had been sleeping facing Bush. She opened her eyes. She quickly shut them.

"Oh," she moaned. "My head is killing me."

Bush was a fairly experienced drinker. Philbrick was a novice. Her mouth was as dry as ordinary shoe leather. Her throat was parched.

"Maybe this will make you feel better," W said. He leaned over. He began kissing his guest. He put his hands around her face. She wrapped her arms around W. They embraced. They kissed for what seemed like the longest time.

"Anyone here?" a voice came from just inside the front door. Philbrick panicked. W jumped up. He threw on his chinos. Philbrick began frantically looking for some clothes. She grabbed one of W's blue, button-down oxford shirts. It was on the back of a chair near the bed.

"Who's there?" W yelled.

"It's your grandmother." Dorothy and Prescott Bush had just arrived. They had driven up from Connecticut. They were anticipating the annual family start-of-summer gathering of the Bush clan. The property was named for her brother.

"Georgie?" she yelled.

"Hi Nanna," he yelled back. "Be right there." He grabbed his Andover letter jacket. He threw it on.

"Jesus, George, what should I do?" Philbrick asked. She was in a panic.

"Sit there and look pretty," he replied.

"George" -- She tried to reply. She couldn't finish her sentence. W had walked out of the room. He needed to cut his grandmother off at the pass, so to speak. He didn't want his grandparents coming to the bedroom.

"Hi Gramp," W said to his grandfather. He met his grandparents in the front foyer.

"Georgie, what are you doing sleeping so late?" his grandfather asked. This was the retired U.S. Sen. Prescott Bush. He didn't suffer fools gladly. He was stern with his eldest grandson. "You ought to be getting this place ready for your parents."

"Ah, Gramps, I'll get to it," W said. "You guys want some coffee?"

"That would be wonderful, honey," W's grandmother replied. "Georgie, I'll put this in the den," she added. She was referring to her small travel bag.

W's grandmother got to the den. She put her bag down on an upholstered chair. The chair had been in her family for years. This house was a nostalgic place for her. She remembered her younger years. She looked the old place over. She noticed the liquor-cabinet doors were wide open. She saw a bottle of liquor in back of one of the open doors.

"Georgie?" she yelled. "Someone having a party?"

"Why Nanna?" he replied.

"I see the liquor cabinet is open," she said.

"Oh, that," W said. He walked in to the den. "Nah, well, not really."

"George W. Bush," his grandmother said. "I hope you're not drinking your father's expensive liquor."

"No Nanna," he replied. "Only the cheap stuff."

"Georgie, you know what I meant," she said.

"Yeah, I know," he said. "Only a little Jim Beam."

"Hi," Philbrick said to W's grandparents. She came from his bedroom. She looked like she just woke up.

"Oh, hi," Dorothy Bush said.

"Nanna, you remember Miss-fit," W said.

"I'm Missy Philbrick," she said to Dorothy Bush. She extended her hand. "We met briefly last summer."

"Oh yes," Dorothy Bush said. "Missy Philbrick. Georgie, what did you call her?"

"Miss-fit, Nanna," W replied. "It's her nickname."

"Oh, I see," his grandmother said. She raised her eyebrows as only a grandmother can do.

His grandparents settled in. W realized he had to attend to something – the damaged Whaler. Senior would be in town by the weekend. Junior knew if the boat weren't ready, there would be hell to pay. Bush walked in to the kitchen. He was about to call the boatyard. Philbrick struck her head in.

"W, I gotta get going," she told him. "My parents are gonna be wondering where I am." She walked back to his bedroom. She got dressed. She saw the two glasses. Each still had a smattering of Jim Beam in them. She realized she needed to get those glasses to the kitchen sink as quickly as possible. She picked up the glasses. She headed to the kitchen. Junior was there on the phone. He'd reached the boatyard.

She approached the sink. She was going to rinse out the glasses. W took one from her hands. He took a drink. He emptied the glass into his mouth. He handed the empty glass to Philbrick. He took the other one from her other hand. He drank its contents. He was smiling. He was quite proud of his prank.

"George, you're nuts," Philbrick said. She was aghast. After all, she was still suffering from a hangover. Her head hurt. She was dehydrated. And here was George W. Bush celebrating the moment. It was before noon. It, before breakfast. He'd already had a couple of sips of bourbon.

"Ah, Miss-fit, you gotta live for the moment," W told her. Then, into the phone, he said, "Yeah, it's Bush. George Bush."

"Oh, Mr. Bush, hi," said Timmy Crane. Crane was a mechanic at the boatyard. "How ya' doin'?"

"OK, Timmy," W replied. "By the way, this isn't my father. It's me, you know, W."

"Yeah, I thought so," Crane replied. "What can I do ya out of?"

"Well," W replied, "I got a little problem. One, I need some Beer Nuts to go with my drink. And two, the prop on the Whaler is mangled. My father is due this weekend. He'll kill me."

"I can help you with the prop," Crane said. "Dunno 'bout the Beer Nuts, but we'll do the best we can."

"Cool," W replied. "You wanna swing by and take a look at the prop? Or should I trailer it over to you."

"No, hell no, we'll swing by and take a look at 'er," Crane said. "Someone gonna be there this afternoon?"

"Oh sure," W replied. "But don't worry if no one's here. Make yourself at home. Do whatever you need to do. If I'm out on a beer run, I'll catch up with you later."

"Sounds good," Crane said. He was laughing. "OK, Mr. Bush. I don't see no problem. I think we can probably change it right there. I'll bring an extra prop with me."

"OK thanks Bubba," W said, The nickname fit the cause. "Talk to ya' later."

They each hung up.

"George, I'll see you later," Philbrick said.

"How you gonna get home?" W asked.

"On foot," Philbrick said.

"No way Jose," W replied. "I'll run you over in the Jeep - so to speak."

"But it's not registered," Philbrick said. "Register this," W said, pointing at his crotch. "Come on, let's go."

Philbrick shook her head in amazement. W had just had a few sips of Jim Beam. He hadn't had any breakfast. He was now ready to hop back the Jeep. It was just hours after he got a traffic ticket for failing to have a license plate. He'd just gotten a warning for speeding. He and Philbrick left the house. W yelled to his grandparents, "See ya' in a few minutes," he said. "Gonna run Miss-fit home." He and Philbrick walked over to the Jeep. Its top was still down. W hadn't raised it after the vehicle had been towed back to the house.

"Hop in," he instructed her. He turned the ignition on. He pushed the starter switch. The old beast chugged and spit. It finally caught. Bush pushed in the clutch. He caught first gear. He screamed down the driveway. The Jeep's rear tires were spinning. They were burning rubber. They were making a tremendously loud screeching sound.

"What in good God was that?" Dorothy Bush said to her husband. She was unpacking their bags. "Oh, I have one good idea," U.S. Sen. Prescott Bush replied to his wife. "Our grandson."

"I wonder if his mother knows about this," Dorothy Bush wondered aloud. "Can you imagine? If his father had ever done that he would have had hell to pay."

Prescott Bush was once a teenager himself. He shook his head. He laughed. He also surmised that his boy, George H.W. Bush, might well have behaved similarly in his adolescence. In fact, he probably had.

W pulled out of his parents' driveway. He took a left turn. He nearly tipped the Jeep over. Philbrick was holding the grab bar. The bar was in front of her seat. She held on with both hands. W started trying to open the glove compartment. He wanted to see if he'd left a pack of Camels in there. He stretched to try to find his cigarettes. He lost control of the steering wheel. He veered off the right side of the road. He went on to the dirt shoulder. He almost hit a young boy. The boy was riding his bicycle and being chased by his dog.

"W slow down!" Philbrick yelled. She also grabbed his right arm. She tried to pull it out of the glove box.

"No sweat, Miss-fit," he told her. "Problem is, no cigarettes, either. Damn." He pulled back his arm. He began turning right. He was headed toward Philbrick's parents' house.

"Should we run that cat over?" W asked Philbrick.

"No!" she yelled. The Jeep was headed for a cat. The cat was nestled in the tall grass beside the road.

"A good cat is a dead cat," W proclaimed. He was laughing. He headed for the cat. Philbrick grabbed the wheel with her left hand. She tried to turn the Jeep to the left. They - make that she - avoided killing the cat. But what she wondered was whether W would have spared its life. That's how unpredictable he was. In her eyes he was a loose cannon.

Chapter V
Fresh Man
at Yell University

George H.W. Bush went to Yale. He captained its baseball team. It seemed only natural for his eldest son to be availed of the same opportunity. George W. Bush was also the grandson of former U.S. Sen. Prescott Bush.

Since its founding in 1701, Yale University in New Haven, Conn., has been one of the world's preeminent schools. Its mission stated or unstated - always trying to outdo Harvard. Harvard is its arch-rival.

"All freshmen please report to the orange rug," came the announcement over the PA system at Davies Hall. The new freshman dorm on campus opened the year W began trying to uphold the Bush name at Yale University. Bush was in his room at the time the announcement came over the speaker. The speaker was in the hallway just outside his door. W left his room. He walked the less-than 75 yards to the lobby of Davies Hall. The famous orange rung was located there. The bright, colorful rug was considered the meeting spot of the dorm. The dorm was attached to two women's dorms. The women's dorms were called Winger and Wilkes halls. Dozens of students converged at the orange rug. They included men and women. W began taking in the stock of young females. They would now would be living just a stone's throw from his first-floor room at Davies Hall.

"What's up?" he said to one woman. "I'm George Bush, George W. Bush. You can call me W."

Laurie Schoenfeld introduced herself. "Hi," she said shyly. "Where are you from?"

"Right here, kiddo - New Haven," W replied. "I'm a local original. Know where we can get some beer?"

"No," Schoenfeld said, She laughed. She looked downward. She stared at the orange rug.

"You goin' to the freshman mixer?" W asked her?

"I don't know," she said. "When is it? Is it tonight?"

"Yeah, over at the gym on the other side of campus," W replied.

"Oh, well, maybe," Schoenfeld said. "I hadn't thought much about it. But maybe it's a good idea."

"Excuse me, could I have everyone's attention," said Joel Steiner. He was one of the graduate students who oversaw some of the dorms. "Excuse me?" Finally, the noisy chatter quieted down. Steiner continued his announcement. "Welcome to all of you," he said. "We want you to have a good year here. If I can do anything to help you please let me know."

Bush was standing near the rear of the crowd. He started rolling his eyes. "Cut me some slack," he muttered to himself. He couldn't abide this speech about dormitory success.

"I'm going to hand out some copies of our rules and regulations," Steiner added. "I'll stick around for awhile in case any of you have any questions. You'll also be getting your meal cards and combinations to your mailboxes. They are located right next to the front reception desk."

Steiner began passing out the copies of dorm regulations. The list reached W toward the back of the group. A student handed W a stack of the regulations. "Pass 'em on," the student told Bush. Bush took him at his word. He passed the stack on to someone standing next to him. He didn't take one for himself. "Do you want a copy?" the student asked him.

"Copy this," W replied.

Bush did get a meal card, however. He also got the combination to mailbox #104. Meals and mail - two of the staples of any freshman's life. Beyond the first priorities, beer and cheap wine.

The organizational meeting ended. Bush headed back to his room. He was rooming with another student. The other student was from New Haven. His name was Dan Grant. He was very bright. He and Bush knew each other as children. "Any idea where we can get some beer?" W asked when Grant showed up.

"Dunno," Grant said. "Maybe we can get someone to buy for us downtown. Maybe an upper classman." Bush's family had lived near the campus when he was a kid. He knew the area very well. He decided to take a walk down to the main highway. The highway was near the campus. He was thirsty. He wanted to see if he could get something to drink.

"I'm gonna get some refreshments," he told Grant. "Want anything?"

"Sure, what the hell," Grant said. "Here's some money." He gave Bush $5.He told Bush, "Anything - beer, wine, whatever."

Bush left the room. He ran down a short flight of stairs. The stairs led to the parking lot. The lot was in front of the dorm. It was a bright, sunny, fall day. It was perfect weather for a walk down to the nearby variety store. Bush figured he'd get maybe some wine for himself. It would be a good tonic to prepare him for the freshman mixer. The mixer was an annual dance for freshmen. The event was designed to help them get to know others in their class. Bush saw the mixer as did many a freshman male. "It's a chance to get laid," he said.

Bush got to the main drag. He crossed the street. He headed to a familiar convenience store. It was called Shimmy's Variety. It had a reputation of being "easy." Bush pulled open one of the large all-glass doors on the refrigerators. Bush saw the owner, Shimmy Chase. Chase was behind the counter. Chase was always in the store. He got to know the regulars. Chase had boys about the same age as Bush. He knew that Bush was not of legal age to buy alcohol. But Chase also felt that if he denied too many youngsters the chance to buy beer or wine, his profits would suffer.

"Hey W," said Chase. He was a large, overweight, man. He showed his ever-present big, broad smile. "What ya' up to today?

"Planning to chase some women, Mr. Chase," W replied, laughing heartily. "Hoping to go to the freshman mixer tonight. Should be worth a shot, huh?"

"You got it," Chase said. W went over to the huge floor-to-ceiling beer coolers. They were located on the rear wall of the store. Bush pulled out a six-pack of his favorite cheap beer, Knickerbocker. He also grabbed a bottle each of Boone's Farm Apple Wine and Bali Hai. He headed for the check-out counter. He stopped on the way to grab a box of Chitos. To Bush they were "She-toes."

"Let's see what we got here," Chase said. Bush put his stuff on the counter. Chase rung up the beer, two bottles of wine and the snacks. He put all the loot in a brown grocery bag. He never asked Bush for identification to prove he was of legal age to buy alcohol. Of course, Chase rarely if ever asked for

ID cards. He sold to just about anybody. In this case, he knew W was not of age. "Enjoy your mixer," Chase laughed. Bush lifted the big heavy bag. He headed for the door.

"Will do," W replied to Chase. "I'll let you know if I score a whore."

Bush began walking back to the dorm. He was eager to get the party underway. "Hell, why wait," he said to himself. He crossed the main drag. He pulled a beer from the bag. He popped the top. He took a big swig. He was out in public. Anyone could see what he was doing – illegally. It illegal for him to buy beer. It was illegal for him to possess it. It was illegal for him - anyone for that matter, regardless of age - to drink alcohol in public. Never bothered W before. Why should it now? And, "damn, that tastes good," he exclaimed out loud as he took his first big swallow of cold Knickerbocker. Bush still had a beer in his hand. He arrived at the dorm. He considered putting the beer back in the bag. If he did he would not have drawn attention to himself. But he quickly realized that would be just a little too much. His attitude - grab for it when you can. He took another big gulp. He approached the front doors of Davies Hall.

"Hey W," his roommate and old friend, Dan Grant, said. He ran into Bush on the stairs. "Bring some for me?"

"Kiss what?" W replied, laughing. "No, come on up, we'll get drunk. You goin' to the mixer tonight fag?"

"Wish I were," Grant replied, "Probably gotta hang out with the little woman." Grant was referring to his girlfriend. Gretchen Stark also grew up in New Haven. She was attending a university nearby. She and Grant had been a couple since their high-school years.

W. got to the top of the front stairs. He headed to his room. He opened the door. He went over to the small refrigerator. It was the same one he had at Andover. He put aside the opened beer he had been drinking. He placed the remaining five beers in the refrigerator. He also put in the two bottles of wine. He closed the refrigerator door. He grabbed his open beer. He settled back in a chair next to the big picture window. The window was at the far end of the room. The window overlooked the front entrance. It also overlooked the parking lot to Davies Hall. He turned on his eight-track Radio Shack tape player. The player had been a gift from his grandparents. They bought it for him when he graduated from Andover. He put in his favorite tape - Gary Puckett and the Union Gap. His favorite song was "You're A Woman Now." It was getting close to dinner. Bush figured he might get dressed for the mixer. He could then head over to the dining hall. He could get some dinner there. Gary Puckett and the Union Gap's best tunes were blaring as background music. W finished his beer.

He took the can in his right hand. He arched his right arm. He prepared for a shot into the small metal wastebasket. The basket was across the room. The can rose high. It arched. It dropped. It hit the wastebasket with a loud bang. Bush pumped the air with his right fist. He headed over to the refrigerator. "Hmmmm," he mumbled to himself. "It might just be time for some Boone's Farm." He reached for the green bottle of Boone's Farm Apple Wine. He removed it from the refrigerator. He unscrewed the top. He took a big swig. He liked the taste. He once told a friend it was "just like drinking apple juice." He sat down in the chair. His wine bottle was in hand. The Union Gap was playing. He grabbed the "pig book." The publication contained photos of all freshmen. He would scan the pictures of women. He saw it as work of preparation for the mixer. It was more preparation than he typically had done before any of his final exams at Andover. Maybe it's why he called himself an average student. A half-hour had passed. W figured he would get ready for the big party. He put down the bottle of wine. He went to the closet. He scanned for something to wear to the mixer. He settled on a navy blue blazer, checked slacks, blue Oxford-cloth button-down shirt and a red club tie from Andover. He figured he'd wear his cowboy boots to finish off his wardrobe. He removed the blazer, slacks, shirt and tie from the close. He placed the clothes on the bed. He put the boots on the floor next to the bed. He grabbed the wine. He took another big gulp. He took off the t-shirt and chinos he'd been wearing.

"Shit, guess I'll grab a shower," he said to himself. He took a bath towel from the radiator in the room. He wrapped it around himself. He headed for the door. Not too late for a drink on the way out, he decided. He picked up the bottle of wine. He took a nice big drink.

"Hey guy," he said to someone he ran in to in the hallway. He was on the way to the bathroom. "Party in your pants later, guy." Whomever he was directing his comments at looked at W and started laughing. "Bush, George W.," Bush said to the stranger. He extended his right hand.

"Sperry Waterman," the other person said to W. Waterman extended his hand to shake W's. "Did you say something about a party?"

"Yeah, in your pants guy," Bush replied. He laughed. He could see that Waterman was stumped.

"Just kidding, Waterboy," Bush said. "Don't sweat it. Stop by 104 in a few minutes. I've got some beer and wine."

"Oh, wow, thanks," Waterman replied. He was a bit stunned by Bush's approach Bush was cocky.

Bush walked in to the bathroom. He went over to the bank of tiled shower stalls. He pulled back the beige muslin curtain on one of the showers. He turned on the hot water. Then he turned on the cold water. He removed his towel wrap. He tossed it on the floor. He hopped in the shower. He was feeling the effects of the beer and wine. He almost fell asleep standing beneath the refreshing stream of warm water in the shower. He suddenly realized he'd been in the shower a seemingly long time. He shut off the water. He got out of the shower. He began toweling off. He heard someone walk in to the bathroom.

"Hey, Bush," he heard someone call out. "Where's the party?"

Bush looked out from behind the towel. He saw the young man he had just met. It was Sperry Waterman. "Oh, it's Waterboy!" W exclaimed. "Party in your pants. Gimme a minute. Meet me in my room, 104. I got some stuff on ice."

"Excellent," Waterman replied. "Let's get it on."

Bush finished drying off. He headed from the bathroom to his room. He entered the room. Waterman was there. "Grab a beer from the 'frig," W told him. "Time's a wastin' Waterboy."

Waterman went over to the refrigerator. He opened the door, revealing the Knickerbocker and two bottles of wine. One of them was half gone. "OK if I grab a Knick?" Waterman asked.

"Go for it Waterboy," W replied. "Gimme the Boone's Farm."

Waterman handed Bush the half-drunk bottle of Boone's Farm. At that point, W unscrewed the cap. He took a big swig. "Man, that's nasty," Bush said. "Nasty and nice." Bush started getting dressed for the big night. He threw on his slacks and shirt. He put on his tie and jacket. He finished off the wardrobe with his cowboy boots. This was vintage W. He was half-New Englander, half-Texan. He looked in the mirror over his bureau. He began tying his tie. The bottle of Boone's Farm was now on top of the bureau. He took a drink as he finished up his tie.

"Hey Waterboy, wanna grab some chow?" W asked his new friend.

"Sounds like a plan," Waterman said. He took a swig from the can of Knickerbocker. "Hey, gimme that damn thing," he added. He reached for the bottle of Boone's Farm.

"Be careful Waterboy," W warned. "That's an adult drink."

"What's with this Waterboy jazz?" Waterman asked. "The name's Waterman."

"Waterboy to you guy," W replied. He grabbed the wine bottle. "Let's get some chow."

W capped the Boone's Farm bottle. He kneeled to place it in the refrigerator. Waterman tipped the can of Knickerbocker to his mouth. He emptied its contents.

"Let's go," W said. "Can't leave those babes waitin' at the mixer."

They headed out the door. They descended the steps to the main lobby. They headed for the reception desk. That was the so-called "orange rug" section of the lobby. They went out the door. They headed toward the nearest dining hall. They arrived at the dining hall. They entered the front door. A woman was standing behind the hall's reception desk.

"'Evenin' chick," W said. Waterman winced. He squeezed his eyes shut. Bush extended his hand. He introduced himself to the woman. "Bush, George W.," he said. He smiled. "Glad to meet ya'."

"Margery Egan," the woman replied. She extended her hand.

"You boys heading in for some dinner?" Egan asked.

"It's men-boys to you chickie," W replied. He was laughing hysterically. "You gonna be at the mixer tonight?"

"Would be if I were a freshman, Mr. Bush," Egan replied.

"Oh, you still in high school?" W asked.

"Keep on moving, boys," Egan said. She shook her head. She was disgusted.

W and Waterman got to the dinner line. They flashed their meal cards. The attendant let them through.

"Thank you boys," the attendant said. "Enjoy your meals."

"Men-boys," W corrected. The attendant rolled her eyes. She said nothing.

W. reached for two plastic trays. He told Waterman, "Let's eat and get the hell out of here. Mixer's on tap." They both settled for the Italian offering of the night. They selected the spaghetti and meat balls.

"Big balls," W commented to Waterman. "What I'd give..."

They took their seats at an empty table. W sprinkled some dehydrated grated cheese on his dinner. He then threw a sprinkling of the cheese on Waterman's dinner. He didn't stop first to ask whether he wanted any. "Gotta spice up those balls, Waterboy," W said.

The two ate their dinner quickly. "Come on Waterboy, let's blow this joint," W said. "We'll head back to the room. Awful thirsty." He got up from the table. Waterman was still eating. Waterman chewed his last mouthful. He got up to follow Bush. They left the dining hall. They headed out past the reception area. "Catch ya' at the mixer," W said to Egan. "Bring your friends. Party in 104 now if you wanna come over."

"Thanks but no thanks," Egan replied.

They got to the room. Bush and Waterman went in. Waterman closed the door. Bush headed straight to the refrigerator. "Drink up Waterboy," W said. He tossed a beer to his new drinking buddy.

"Thanks," Waterman said. He wanted to one-up Bush with the nickname-thing. But, as the saying goes, you've either got it or you don't.

Bush uncapped the Boones Farm. He took a big drink. He removed the bottle from his mouth. He started feeling a tad dizzy. It passed after a moment. He took another swig.

"I think I'm good for a nap," Waterman said to Bush. "Guess I'll head back to my room. Might see ya' over at the mixer. OK to take my beer with me?"

"'Course, Waterboy. Drink up. Catch ya' in a while crocodile."

Waterman left the room. He closed the door behind him. Bush sat down on the edge of the bed. His bottle of Boone's Farm was within easy reach. He was all dressed up for the mixer. He was feeling a little sick to his stomach. He closed his eyes. He hung his head. He was hoping the nauseous feeling would go away. W woke up. He looked at the clock. It said 7:30. He realized he had fallen asleep on the side of the bed. He was still dressed for the mixer, of course. There's no time like the present. So he got up. His head was hurting. He picked up the bottle of Boone's Farm. He prepared to head out the door to the mixer. He was putting the bottle of wine in the refrigerator. He said to himself, "One for the road, sucker." He took a big swig of the now-warm wine. He capped the bottle. He put it in the 'frig. He left his room. He walked down the front stairs. He went out the door. He took a left to head over to the gym. It was a nice fall night, albeit a bit brisk. That's what the wine was for - to warm him up. It would help in more ways than one.

Bush was walking toward the gym. He noticed that he was having a little trouble maintaining his gait. He seemed to find it hard to walk a straight line. He didn't pay undue notice to the issue. He was more focused on getting to the mixer. He wanted to, well, mix it up a bit with some freshman chicks. He got to the traffic island in front of the gym. He noticed a lot of people milling about the front entrance. He walked in the door. Suddenly heard a lot of loud noise. He heard music. He heard the combined cacophony of thousands of people talking. The room started spinning. Bush knew he was in trouble. He somehow made his way immediately out the front door. He walked about 50 feet. He ended up in the middle of the traffic island. His legs turned to rubber. He realized he had to get to the ground. He lay down on his back. His feet were splayed out in front of him. They were nearly sticking out into the pavement where cars would turn around after dropping passengers off at the front door of the gym. He was feeling quite dizzy. And sick. He held his head and began moaning. He closed his eyes. "Somebody help me," he said. "Somebody help me."

He repeated the same phrase over and over again. In his drunken stupor he expected some kind soul would heed his pleas. Someone would hopefully help this drunken freshman from his nauseating plight. A few minutes passed. Bush felt like he was passing in and out of consciousness. Someone bent down. "What do you need?" Bush heard a young woman say to him. "I'm sick drunk," W replied. "Had a bit too much to drink. That fucking Boone's Farm does it to me every time."

"What can I do?" the woman asked.

"Gimme a big kiss," W replied. He was slurring his words. "Come." He reached out with his arms. He tried to embrace the woman.

"Well, we need to get you up," the woman said.

"That's the whole point," W wisecracked. "I don't know if I can get up in the condition I'm in. Hey what's your name?"

"Diane," she said.

"Diane who?" he asked.

"Diane Longyear," she replied.

"I long for you," W replied.

"Come on, let's see if we can get you up, on your feet," Longuir said.

"Good luck girl," he replied.

She began trying to help him on to his feet. He started moaning. He fell back to the ground. "Come on," she urged. "Let's try again. What's your name?"

"George," he said.

"George?" she replied. "That's a nice name."

"Screw George," Bush replied. "I hate my name. Call me anything but George. My last name is Bush, you know, Bush. You got a bush?"

"OK," Longyear said. She decided this wasn't a discussion for the moment. "Let's see if we can make some progress here." She again began trying to help him up off the ground. She had a bit more success this time. But he was heavy in her arms. She was having a lot of trouble lifting him up. He felt like deadweight. He was doing little to help her because he was so drunk. "OK, we're making some progress, George," she said.

"Don't call me George," he slurred. "Georgie Boy. Or Stud. Or GB. Not George." In his drunken state, W was all about broadcasting his apparent resentment at having been named the same thing as his father.

"OK, whatever," Longyear said. "Come on, help me get you up." Finally she got Bush on his feet. He was covered with grass and mud. His tie was all askew.

"Can you walk me back to the dorm?" he slurred. "Right down there." He pointed toward the direction of where Davies Hall was located.

"OK," Longyear said. "Hey Margo," she yelled to a friend. "I'm gonna help this guy back to his dorm. I'll be back."

"OK Di," her friend, Margo Foulds, yelled back from a group of freshmen girls. The group was gathered in a small circle outside the gym. They were smoking. "Be careful. You OK?"

"Yeah," Longyear answered. "I just need to help him. I think he had a little too much to drink."

"Don't say the word drink," W slurred. He tried to smile. "Please, don't say that word right now."

"OK," Longyear said. "Let's start walking now. You with me?"

"Yeah," W replied. "I can't thank you enough for helping me. What's your name again?"

"Diane," she replied.

"Oh yeah, Diane," he said. "That's a nice name. Diane who?"

"Diane Longyear," she said.

"Oh yeah," he replied. "That's right again. Longyear. This is gonna be a Long year alright. I can't thank you enough for helping me."

"No problem," Longuir said. "You feeling any better?"

"No," he said. "Are we almost there?"

"Yeah, the dorm is right there," she said. She pointed to the dorm. They got to the front door. They walked in. Bush pointed to show her which way his room was. They got to room 104. Bush reached into his right front pants pocket for the key. He put the key in the door. He opened it. He virtually collapsed on the bed.

"Write down your name and phone number on my desk so I can thank you later," Bush slurred.

"OK," Longyear said. She found a pen and some scrap paper on the desk. It was near the bunk bed. She wrote down her name and number. "Hope you feel better," she said. She touched her fingers to his forehead to check his temperature.

"Thanks chickie," W replied. "Really 'preciate your helping me out. Talk to you later."

Longyear opened the door. She left the room. She headed back to the mixer. Bush fell asleep. He was still completely dressed.

He woke up hours later. He was sitting on the floor of his dorm room. He was covered in vomit. Bush had gotten sick. He had thrown up all over his bed and his clothes. It was now just before 3 a.m.. The door to his room opened. It was Dan

Grant, his roommate. Grant was returning from a night of romp and circumstance.

"Jeezus," Grant said. "What the hell you been in to?"

"Don't," Bush begged. He tried to hold his head up. "Don't."

Grant grabbed a bath towel. He took it to the bathroom. He stuck it in the sink and soaked it with water. He came back to the room. He tossed it to Bush. Bush started wiping the vomit from himself. "Man this stinks," he said. He tried to get up from the floor. He fell back down. His head was throbbing. He was too weak to move. He fell asleep as he sat on the floor. He had a wet towel in his lap. His clothes stunk from vomit.

So much for the mixer.

Bush was hoping to meet a few prospects. But the Boone's Farm put a bit of a damper on his plans.

The sun came up Saturday morning. It shone brightly into the dorm room. George W. Bush opened his eyes briefly. He closed them just as quickly. He was sleeping in. He was nauseous. His head was killing him. He was parched.

"Hey boy want something to eat?" Bush heard someone say. He looked up. It was Waterman.

"Hey Waterboy," Bush moaned. He looked up from beneath his covers. "Eat? Oh man, I don't think I can eat right now."

"Come on you old fart, get up," Waterman said. "What's the matter? Drink too much last night?"

"Don't say the word drink," Bush pleaded. It was almost noon. He decided he'd like to try to get out of bed. He pushed himself up. He fell back to the bed. He was in agony. He took a deep breath. He tried again to get up. He hung his head. His eyes closed. He tried to muster the energy he needed if he wanted to do something other than stay in bed all day. He squeezed his eyes. He braced for the next effort. He finally was able to assume a sitting position. His head still hung low. His head hurt. He was nauseous. He remained that way for what seemed like the longest time.

Waterman had since left the room. He left the door open. Bush liked the door open. He enjoyed people - even strangers - stopping by or exchanging greetings. He was writhing in agony. He tried to get up from the bed. He saw something out of the corner of his eye. It was someone standing in the doorway. "Heard you were under the weather," said a man. He was leaning against the door jam. "Can I get you a cold beer?"

"Oh my god," W replied. "What the fuck are you trying to do to me?"

"Come on, get up," the man said. "Time to start the weekend. I'm Leon Bisson. I live down a few doors. Tryin' to get a few guys together tonight for a party."

"Party farty," W replied. He moaned. "Shit, I gotta get out of this crap." He looked down at his vomit-stained clothes. His blazer and pants were covered. They stunk. He slowly pulled off his blazer. He tossed it in the corner. Then he started, button...by...button...by...button ...by...button, slowly taking off his shirt.

Then his pants. S-l-o-w-l-y. He moved like he was in s-l-o-w m-o-t-i-o-n.

"Throw me that towel, Peon," W said. He was weak.

"Leon," Bisson said. He fetched the towel. "It's Leon."

"That's what I said, Peonboy," W replied. He smiled weakly. He took the towel. He threw it back at Bisson. He grabbed it back. "See ya' in a minute," he told Bisson. He walked out the door. He was moaning in agony. The hangover was vicious. He walked to the bathroom. It was down the hall. He went in and headed for the showers. He turned on the hot water. Then the cold water. He got in. He put his face directly in the powerful stream of water. Bush stood frozen for minutes. He started thinking of ways to get over the hangover. "I think I need a beer," he said to himself. He was shaking from alcohol withdrawal. He was dehydrated. He shut off the shower. He stood motionless in the stall. He was shivering. His skin was covered with goose bumps. Suddenly he felt his stomach giving way. He started retching. He was heaving. He quickly turned on the shower head again. Suddenly he heaved a mouthful of vomit. It splashed on the floor of the shower stall. Bush was swallowing hard. He tried to stop vomiting. He started retching violently. He couldn't produce more vomit. He bent over. He rested his hands on his knees to support the weight of his torso. The water from the shower head was hitting him on the back of his neck. He stayed in that position for several minutes. He tried to regain himself.

Time... dragged... on...

Bush was so, so sick.

He found the courage to try to get from his hunched-over position into an upright position. He fell sideways against the back right corner of the shower stall. He reached for the faucets. He was able to shut off the water. He leaned back against the wall in shivering silence.

He approached the doorway of the shower. He reached to pull back the curtain. He reached for his towel. He cried out in agony. He was nauseous. He was in pain. He wanted to be dead.

Death couldn't come soon enough. Death would be a gift. He started blotting his face with the towel. "Please God, help me," W asked.

Faith was nice. But it didn't do much to help a ghastly hangover.

Bush dragged himself out of the shower. He sat down on the cold, tile threshold. He hung his head between his legs. His eyes closed. The towel was draped across his knees and thighs. Someone entered the bathroom. Bush didn't have the energy to look up to see who it was. He didn't care who it was. The next thing he heard was a door to one of the toilet stalls close. He heard someone unbuckling his pants. Then he heard someone farting, passing gas.

"Shut the fuck up," Bush yelled.

"Fuck off," the voice from the stall replied.

"Who the fuck is that?" Bush asked.

"Your mama," the voice said.

"Eat shit," Bush replied.

"You'd like to," said the voice in the stall. Bush was able to get to his feet. He shuffled to the bathroom door. He opened it. He walked out into the hallway. The linoleum-over-concrete floor was cold and refreshing on his feet. He got to the door of his room. He walked in. He sat down on the edge of his bed. He was motionless. He breathed slowly. His head was throbbing.

"Ready for a beer?" he heard someone ask.

Bush didn't look up. He just shook his head. "Come on, W," the voice said, "let's rally." The man leaned down. He put his right hand on Bush's left shoulder.

Bush looked up. It was Leon Bisson.

"Peonboy," Bush said weakly.

"Come on," Bisson said. "You'll be OK. We just gotta get something in you. I'm gonna get you a coffee in the machine. I'll be right back." Bisson left Bush. He walked down the hall to the game room. The vending machines and a ping-pong table were located there. He dropped 25 cents into one machine. He pushed the button for a black coffee. He returned with it to Bush's room. "Here, try this," Bisson said. He handed Bush the paper cup with black coffee.

"Thanks Peon," W said weakly. He extended his left hand to receive the cup. Bush took a sip of the coffee. A few minutes later he took another sip. "Hey Peon, can you get me some water?" Bush asked. Bisson took a glass from Bush's desk. He went to fill it up at the water fountain down the hall.

"Here ya' go," Bisson said. He handed Bush a glass of cold water. Bush took a sip. He put the glass on the floor. A half hour passed. Bush was able to slip some clothes on - chinos, button-down shirt, loafers. Bisson brought him some ice cream from another vending machine.

"Thanks Peon," W said. "You're a pal."

"Hey, wait 'til I introduce you to Cindy Tillotson," Bisson replied.

"Who's that?" W asked.

"I'm fixing you up with her tonight," Bisson said. "I thought you, me, John Bourland and John McCown would head to Milford. My parents aren't around so we can use the house. Can we use your father's car?"

"Yeah," W replied. He took a sip of coffee.

It was just before 4 p.m. W awoke from a nap. He was still feeling a little woozy. He felt far better than he had several hours earlier. "Ready to rumble?" Bisson asked. He peered his head in the door. "Bourland and McCown are on their way."

W got up and stretched. "What are we doing for beer Peon?" he asked Bisson.

"I've got a case," Bisson replied. "We can get more when we get to Milford."

W and Bisson headed for the parking lot. Bush had parked his father's car there earlier. They met Bourland and McCown. The four hopped in and left for Milford. "What's with this chick you're fixing me up with?" W asked. "Hey, gimme a beer."

"Here," Bisson said. "Drink in good health." He handed W a cold Pabst Blue Ribbon. Bush took his right hand off the wheel. He popped the can. "Here's to solving a hangover," he said. He took a big gulp. "So, Peonboy, what's with this chick?"

"Oh," Bisson laughed. "She's this whore I know. I went to high school with her. She's a lot of fun." He laughed hard.

Bush had yet to lose his virginity. He was excited. To quell his nerves, he figured he'd have a few beers. By the time he met his date, he'd be more relaxed. He pulled into the Bisson's driveway. The four men got out of the car. They went into the house. Bisson went into the basemen. From a storage refrigerator he pulled two six-packs of beer. He and his father kept their stash in the basement refrigerator. The Bissons were a drinking, working-class family. They were unlike Bush. He grew up in a white-collar clan.

W grabbed another beer. He toasted Bisson, Bourland and McCown. "Here's to three assholes," Bush said, "and to me getting laid tonight."

"Speaking of assholes," Bourland told W, "make sure you don't get confused."

"Fuck off Bouring-boy," W replied. It was just after 6:30 p.m. Each of the men had had a few beers. The gang figured they'd hop in Bush's father's car. Time to pick up the girls.

"Take a sip of this first," Bisson told W. He handed him a glass.

Bush took the glass. He downed its contents. "Gag me!" W said. "What the hell was that?"

"Good old Kentucky bourbon," Bisson said. He was laughing.

W was feeling pretty good now, in more ways than one. He opened the driver's door of his father's car. He got in. He started the car. Bisson sat to his right. The other two got in the back seat. "We'll pick up my girl," Bisson said. "Then we pick up your date, W."

"OK P-boy," W replied. "You tell me where to go." Bisson directed W to his - Bisson's - girlfriend's house. They stopped to pick her up. From there they headed to pick up Cindy Tillotson. She would be Bush's date. Bush and Bisson got out of the car and went to the door.

"Oh hi," Tillotson said when she opened the door.

"Cindy, I'd like you to meet George Bush," Bisson said. "He's heard all about you."

"Oh, I bet you have," Tillotson said. She was laughing devilishly. "Nice to meet you George."

"No, everyone calls me W," Bush replied. He took a drink from the beer he was holding. "Nice to meet you, Cinchy, uh, Cindy." He laughed. "If you're in a pinch, call Cinch."

Tillotson was an easy laugh. She grabbed a jacket and bid her mother good-bye. She followed Bush and Bisson to the car. She sat between the two of them. They were in the front seat. Bush backed out of the driveway. He tossed his now-empty beer can out the window. He asked Bourland to hand him another beer.

Bisson directed W to their next stop. They would pick up a couple of more girls. The car crested a steep hill. The road veered to the right and then sharply to the left. W almost lost control of the car. He swerved at one point far over the center line. "Holy shit," W said. He had one hand on the wheel. One hand was holding a can of beer. He handed Tillotson his beer. He would try to concentrate on his driving. "Here, drink this," he said.

"OK," she said agreeably. She tipped the can to her lips and emptied it. "Got any more?" she asked playfully.

"Holy cow," W said. "You sure sucked that down fast."

"You ain't seen nothin' yet," she laughed.

Bourland handed Tillotson another beer. The four headed to their next stop. They picked up two more women. Bush drove the gang back to Bisson's. Bisson had Bush stop at a local variety store. He was always able to buy beer there with no questions asked. They got to Bisson's house. They stashed the two cases of beer they had just bought. They all settled down in the living room for some drinking. Bisson was with his girlfriend. Bourland and McCown were talking to two women they had just met. Bush was sitting in a stuffed chair.

"Make yourself comfortable," he told Tillotson. He motioned her to sit down. She began looking for a chair she could drag over. She wanted to put a chair next to the one in which W was sitting. "Here, this'll work," W said. He suggested she sit on the arm of his chair. Tillotson was a playful sort. She was quite agreeable.

"OK," she chirped. "Just a second. Let me get a beer."

"You've already got a beer Cinchy," W said. He used a nickname that Bisson had explained she got for obvious reasons.

"Yeah, I know," Tillotson chirped. "But I wanna have one on tap, too."

"Oh, one on tap," W replied. "That's very good."

Bush celebrated plays on words. It didn't matter whether he understood the phonetic and grammatical interplay or not. In this case, he was oh-so delighted to hear someone use what he thought was a cute metaphor. It even had a double entendre. What Tillotson meant was that she wanted to have one "on deck." But on tap worked for Bush because of the reverential keg reference.

"So what are you studying?" Tillotson asked George W. Bush.

"Your beautiful eyes," W replied. He made Tillotson giggle. He took a swig on his beer.

"Hey great line George," shouted Bourland. Bourland was half-listening to Bush and Tillotson. He found their sophomoric interplay amusing.

"Fuck off Boring-man," Bush said to Bourland. "Is that where your family got the name Bourland, because they were so boring?"

"That's good, W really impressive."

"So," Tillotson repeated, "what are you studying?"

"Your beautiful lips," Bush replied.

Tillotson giggled again. "Oh, you're so bad," she said.

"Wanna know what I'm studying?" she asked.

"What, my beautiful eyes?" Bush asked.

"No, silly," she said. "I'm going to cosmetology school."

"Oh, wow, so you're gonna be a fortune teller?" Bush asked her.

"No, no, silly," she said. "I'm going to hair-dressing school. I wanna open my own salon."

"Oh, a hair-dresser," W replied. "I get it now. I was thinking cosmetology. You know. Reading the stars."

"No, that's cometology," she said.

"No, you guys. That's astrology," McCown explained.

"Enough of this," W said. "Cindy, want me to get you another beer?"

"Yeah, goody," she said. "I'll come with you."

"You can come with me any time, honey," Bush joked. The two of them arose from their seats. They went to the refrigerator in the Bisson's kitchen.

Bush opened the refrigerator door with his right hand. Tillotson was on his left side. She was near the opening of the door. He kissed her on her right cheek. She smiled. She gave him a kiss on his left cheek. W reached for a can of Pabst He handed it to Tillotson. He gave her another kiss. He reached for a beer. He closed the refrigerator door. They both opened their cans of beer.

"I'm really glad you guys came tonight," Tillotson said. Bush smiled. Tillotson laughed.

"I'm glad you came too," Bush said.

She giggled. Both of them were feeling quite light-headed. Bush was still reeling a bit from his Boone's Farm hangover from the freshman mixer fiasco. He was all the more vulnerable. But he was like any good drunk. He'd forget from one episode to the next how painful benders could be. So he was off to the races. He'd almost finished his beer. It only took him about six minutes to drink it. He decided to reach for another. He opened the refrigerator door.

"You ready for another one?" he asked Tillotson.

"Sure," she said. She was still sipping from the one can she already had.

Bush grabbed a can and handed it to her. He kissed her again. This time it was on the lips. He grabbed a can for himself. He closed the refrigerator door. He popped the top on his can. He gave Tillotson another kiss. He put his left arm around her left shoulder. They began walking from the kitchen back to the living room. On the way they passed a bedroom.

"I gotta lie down," Bush told Tillotson. "I'm feeling a little dizzy." He took her right hand in his left hand. The two of them walked in to the bedroom. "Are you OK," she asked Bush as he sat down on the edge of the bed.

"Yeah, I think so," he replied. "Will you lay down with me?"

Tillotson kicked off her black flats. She got onto the bed. She lay down next to Bush. She lay on her left side. She faced him. She looked into his eyes. He lay on his back. He took his left arm. He slid it around her neck. He drew her to him. He kissed her. She returned the gesture. She put her lips on his. She closed her eyes.

"You OK?" she cooed softly in his left ear.

"Yeah, thanks Cinchy," he replied. He began removing her blouse. She began unbuttoning his shirt. She slipped off her skirt. She loosened Bush's huge cowboy-belt buckle.

"What is this?" she asked. She referred to the huge buckle of a bucking bronco.

"Oh, that's tiny compared to what's underneath it," W replied. He was laughing. He was starting to feel dizzy. He was nodding off. He was in a growing-drunken stupor. "Unzip my fly," he told her. She complied. Tillotson removed her panties. He got on top of her. They were kissing and caressing each other. W took his left hand. He began stroking Tillotson's thighs. She began doing the same to him.

He moved her hand toward the inner side of his thigh. He told her to explore on her own. But W was fading. He was about to celebrate the loss of his virginity. Yet he couldn't perform. He was too drunk.

"Oh, Cinchy," he moaned. "Ohhhhhhh."

"What George?" she whispered. "What George?" He was in a fix. The life of the party was gone. He was about to nod off.

Tillotson wasn't too concerned. There were plenty of losers before George W. Bush. There would be plenty later. He was just another drunken college student. She'd been having sex since she was 14. It was no big deal to this rug rat whether George W. Bush had sex with her.

"Hey what's going on in there?" Bourland yelled from the living room.

"Yeah, what is going on in there," Bisson chimed in.

Bush could only manage a weak response. "Nothing," he said. He slurred the word.

The others laughed.

Bush faded into virtual unconsciousness. Tillotson got up. She sat on the edge of the bed. She put on her clothes. First, her blouse. Then, her underwear. Then, her skirt. Finally, her black flats. She figured she'd let her date sleep off his drunk. She got up. She went into the living room.

Bush's friends were drinking and visiting in the living room. He was napping. Several hours later he opened his eyes, He rubbed his forehead. "Where the fuck am I?" he asked himself. He realized he was in a bedroom. He was at Leon Bisson's house. He was in Milford. He looked at his watch. It said 2:35. He sat up on the edge of the bed. He saw someone lying next to him. He realized it was Cindy Tillotson. She was resting on top of the covers. She had a blanket over her. She woke up.

"Shit. I should get home," she said. "Can you bring me home?"

"Now?" Bush asked. "It's 2:30 in the fucking morning."

"So?" she asked.

"OK, whatever chickie, let's go," he replied. He started getting dressed. His head was throbbing. The living room was full of bodies. Everyone started stirring. "Holy shit, it's 2:30," Bisson said. Bourland, McCown and the other three girls were all sleeping on the floor. Bisson's girlfriend was on the couch.

"Cindy wants me to bring her home," W complained to the crowd. "Anyone else need rides?"

"Why don't we bring all the girls home?" Bisson suggested. "No time like the present." They all got up. They threw on clothes. They prepared to get in Bush's father's car.

"Don't forget the beer," Bisson said. He was serious.

"Please, if I hear that word again I'll puke," W said.

"Hey Cindy, come," he said. He motioned her over to him.

She walked over. "I'd like to," she said.

"Let's get it on tonight," W suggested.

"We'll see what's up," Bisson said. "We've got all day to make plans."

W kissed Tillotson. She kissed him. They all headed for the door.

Everyone piled in the car. Tillotson was ahead of Bush. She slipped in through the driver's door. She sat down beside him.

"Guess I got a little ahead of myself," he told her. He gave her a kiss. "Drank too much."

"I wish you'd drunk me," Tillotson said.

"Good Cinchy," he replied. He started the car. He kissed her. He looked over his right shoulder. He backed out of the driveway. He nearly hit a tree alongside the driveway.

"What's this thing," she asked? She grabbed his crotch. He flinched, laughing hard.

"You can dress me up but you can't take me out," W told Bisson.

Later the next day the men were back in the dorm. They relaxed in the game room at Davies Hall. They played poker, sipping on beer. "I was so drunk last night I couldn't even get it up," W told Bisson.

"You blew the golden moment," Bisson said.

"Blow this," Bush said. He tossing a royal flush on the table.

The card game folded. W and Bisson went back to their respective rooms. W got to his room. His roommate Dan Grant was sitting on his desk. He was talking to someone W hadn't ever seen.

"W, meet Mike Rosenberg," Grant said.

"Glad to meet ya'," Bush said. He extended his hand. "'Can I offer you a beer. Plenty more in the 'frig down here."

"Oh, thanks, actually I'd love one," Rosenberg said.

"Here ya' go," W said. He reached into the refrigerator. "So what's your claim to fame Rosenblatt?"

"Rosenberg," he corrected Bush.

"Rosenberg. Rosenblatt, Rosenstein. They're all the same," Bush replied.

"I'm from one of the fraternities on campus here," Rosenberg explained. He took a seat on the edge of W.'s bed. "This is rush season and each of the houses is trying to recruit new members from the freshman class. I had heard you two guys were from around here so I thought I'd stop by."

"What's it gonna cost us?" Bush asked. He took a swig on his beer. "Don't wanna waste money on rivalrous stuff. Whatever that word is."

"Frivolous," Grant said. "It's frivolous."

"Well, fellas," Rosenberg said, "we don't consider this frivolous. You would pay social dues. That's all it would be. Plus room and board if you live at the house. But you'd be paying for room and board anyway. Ya see?"

"Yeah, that makes sense," W said. "About as much sense as cutting off my right foot. Why would I want to pay social dues? Hell, we make our own parties here. We don't have to pay no dues."

"Well, do me this much," Rosenberg asked. "We're having a keg party Saturday. We'd like to have you fellas come down. See what you think."

"Keg party," W said. "Now we're getting somewhere. Where's this house?"

"It's on South Wollard Street," Rosenberg said. "572 Wollard. Right across the street from that small girls' college."

"OK," W said. "We'll be there. Well, I'll be there. Dunno about Grant. He'll probably be balling his girlfriend somewhere. What's the name of this house again?"

"It's called Delta Kappa Epsilon," Rosenberg said. "DKE. These fraternities, you'll learn, are commonly known by their letters. In our case, it's DKE."

"Kinda like, deek," Bush laughed. "That'll be great. Anyone asks what house are you from? I'll say I'm a deek."

"Well, actually it would be 'dyke,' ' Rosenberg said. "But whatever, deek is fine if you like deek."

"Well, don't get me wrong," W said. "I ain't got nothin' against dykes. Whatever. I get the point."

"OK. You wanna stop by for dinner before the party? It'll be on me," Rosenberg said.

"Oh, OK," Bush said. "Hell, I'll be there. What time?"

"Dinner usually starts around 6," Rosenberg said. "Just come on down and find me. My room is on the second floor. Just come in the front door. Come up the stairs. Take a right. Down the hall. At the end. That's me." After Rosenberg left, W told Grant he thought they should take a chance. Neither of them had ever thought about joining a fraternity. All they knew about fraternities was that during the winter they would build snow-and-ice sculptures outside their houses.

"Good chance to meet some chicks," W said to his room-mate. "Not that you care about meeting chicks." He knew that Grant had a steady girl. He sensed that Grant was getting pretty tired with the same woman. Hell, at age 18, who the hell wants a steady girl?

"I don't know," Grant told W. "Maybe I'll come down with you for the dinner. If I can ditch the old lady, I'll stay for the keg party."

"Excellent," W said. "Deek, here we come."

"No, it's dyke, not deek," Grant said. "Aw screw it, who cares, dyke, deek, suck, screw. Get them kegs tapped, now!"

Classes were out. It was now Friday. W walked back to his dorm. He was wondering if he should stop to buy some beer. He'd been eagerly anticipating the weekend. He always looked forward to weekends. They meant a respite from academics. They also were a chance to throw back some beers. But this weekend was going to be the keg party. At a frat. He hadn't ever been to a keg party at a fraternity house. Now, holy God, he was old enough. He'd actually reached the age when someone was asking him to join a fraternity. He still couldn't legally drink. No matter. No one ever paid attention to what went on at the frat houses. He was George Bush. He did what he wanted anyway. Legal or illegal. Didn't much matter.

He got near the dorm. W figured he'd stop by his room. He'd relax a bit before making a beer run. He knew he had a few cans in the refrigerator. He'd be good for a couple of hours. He got to his room. He heard the phone ringing. Few freshmen had phones in their rooms. This wasn't just any freshman. This was George W. Bush, after all.

"George?"

"Hey Pops," W replied. "What's goin' on?"

"Just wanted to see how school is going," George H.W. Bush said. "You makin me proud?"

"Do bears shit in the woods?" W asked his father. "Hey, how's the campaign going?"

The senior Bush was running in Texas for the U.S. Senate. He was running as a Republican against Ralph Yarborough. Senior was a bit preoccupied with his career. He wasn't connected with his son's academic situation. W's start in college in the fall of 1964 was overshadowed by his father's having to concentrate on his Senate bid.

"We're doin' OK, I think," senior Bush told his namesake. "What's doin' at school?"

"I'm gonna go to a fraternity house tomorrow," W excitedly told his father.

"Oh?" his pop replied. "Which one?"

"Dyke house," W replied.

"You mean deke," his father said.

"Deek, dyke, all the same to me," W said. "They're having a keg party, so it don't matter to me whether they're dykes or dekes."

"Well, I think that's good, son," his father told him. "I had a lot of fun in the Greek system when I was there."

"No, this is deke, not Greek," W said.

"No, son, I understand," his father replied. "The fraternities are part of what's known as the Greek system."

"Oh, gotcha," W said. "All I know is, they say they're gonna have a keg."

"Well, you be careful," his father said. "Don't let your mother know you're drinking."

"What's this I heard - drinking?" Barbara Bush yelled into the kitchen. That's where her husband was talking to his son on the phone. (Make that Barbara's son...)

"Oh, nothing," senior Bush told her.

"Hey, guys, you can argue later without me," W said into the phone. "I gotta run."

"OK, son, take care," Poppy Bush said. "Wait, hold on, your mother wants to say hi."

"Georgie?" she said. She grabbed the phone from her husband.

"Hey Mummsy," W said.

"I heard your father say something about drinking," she replied.

"Oh mummsy, just a fraternity party," her son replied. "No big deal. Just gonna have a few beers tomorrow night."

"I'm suddenly going deaf," his mother said. "Honey, you be a good boy and keep up with your school work."

"OK, Mummsy," W replied. "Talk to you later."

"OK, Georgie. Love ya'," his mom said. "Bye-bye."

He hung up with his parents. W really needed a drink. He reached down to his little refrigerator. He opened the door. He grabbed a can of Pabst. He popped a Leonard Cohen tape in his eight-track player. He kicked off his loafers. He hopped onto his bed. He lay down on his back. He fluffed up the pillow under his head. A beer was safely ensconced in his left hand.

He took a gulp of his bee. George W. Bush gazed from his bed out the large picture window. He was thinking now about one thing. He was thinking about the upcoming keg party at DKE.

"George Bush, paging George Bush, the man who couldn't get it up."

Bush was startled. He looked over his left shoulder. Leon Bisson had walked in. He decided to razz Bush about the latter's date the week before with Cindy Tillotson, the whore of Milford.

"Eat me," W told Bisson.

"You'd like me to," Bisson replied. "Got any more of those?"

"Any more what, Bison-boy?" Bush asked.

"It's Bisson to you, lover boy," Bisson replied.

"It's Bison to me," Bush said. "In the 'frig, asshole."

Bisson opened the 'frig. He grabbed a beer. He sat down in the easy chair. The chair was at the foot of Bush's bed. "You have fun last week with Cindy?" Bisson asked.

"Hey, she's a handful," W said. "Too bad I was too drunk. I couldn't enjoy the moment. Christ, I got her clothes off. Then I went limp. I tried to screw her but nothing happened."

"Did you wash your dick off afterward?" Bisson asked.

"Screw off, Bison-boy," W replied. "So what if it falls off. Hey wanna make a beer run?"

"Yeah. Lemme polish this off. We'll head out," Bisson said. "You can tell me more about Cindy, uh, Cinchy."

Bush sucked down the last remnants of his Pabst. He called it Pabs because he couldn't figure out how to enunciate the triple consonants. He lobbed the empty across the room. It hit the rim of the waste basket. "Fuck," he lamented.

"Loser," Bisson said. "Watch this." He finished his beer in one massive, fell swoop. He launched his empty toward the basket. It went in. "Two points!" Bisson said.

"It was a rim job," Bush replied. "Only one point for rim jobs."

"Hey don't tell me about poor rim jobs," Bisson said. "You had your chance last night and you blew it."

"No," W replied. "She blew it."

The two of them got up and left the room. They headed down to Shimmy's Variety. Time to buy some more beer. They decided to take Bush's father's car. They pulled into Shimmy's lot. W handed Bisson $10. Bisson ran inside while W stayed in the car.

"Afternoon," Shimmy, the owner, said to Bisson.

"Hi Mr. Shimmy," Bisson said.

"Shimmy will do," the owner joked. Bisson went to the coolers. They were at the back of the store. He took out four six-packs. He grabbed two of Pabst and two of Knickerbocker. He went to the counter. He handed Shimmy $10. Shimmy put the loot in two brown grocery bags. Bisson headed out of the store. He got in W's car.

"Gimme one of those, Bison-boy" W said to Bisson.

"Hold your freakin' horses," Bisson said. "Whaddayawant, a Knick' or Pabst?"

"Pabs," W replied. He was backing out of his parking space.

"It's Pabst," Bisson said. He corrected W's pronunciation. "Here ya go." He handed Bush a can of beer.

"It's Pabs to you, B-boy," Bush said. He popped the beer open. He was trying to steer the car out of the lot. "So you wanna come to the keg party tomorrow night?"

"Not sure," Bisson said. "I'll have to see what my girl wants to do."

"Screw her," W said. "Tell her who's boss. You're pussy-whipped. It'll be a great party. I'm gonna head down there early. Have dinner with the guys at the frat. You might as well come with me."

The next day he was nursing a hangover. Same score. W took a shower. He threw on some beige chinos, navy golf shirt and, of course, cowboy boots. He threw a stone-colored golf jacket on. He headed out of the dorm. He decided to walk to the DKE house. It was only about a half-mile away. He put a beer in each pocket of his jacket. He also had the open can he was drinking from. He held the open can close. He was preparing. He wanted to be ready in case he ran into someone who wouldn't want to see it.

He got to DKE house 20 minutes late. He walked in the front door. He didn't see anyone in the hallway or in the living room just off the hallway. The first thing on his mind became looking for a bathroom. He walked down the hall. He took a right. He went down another hallway. He followed that hallway into yet another hallway. He found a bathroom. He tossed his empty beer can into a waste basket. He stood in front of one of the urinals.

"Hey, I'm Dave," said a boy who pulled up to the next urinal. "Dave Rechsler."

"George Bush," W replied. "One of the guys from here said it would be cool to come down for dinner and the keg party. So here I am."

"We're glad you came," Rechsler said.

"That's what she said," W replied.

"Huh?" Rechsler asked.

"Nothing," W said in disgust. He was unimpressed that this frat rat would ask what the hell W meant by his wisecrack.

"On well, follow me downstairs," Rechsler said. "We'll get some dinner. Where you from?"

"Here," W said. "I mean New Haven."

"Oh, you're a local boy?" Rechlser asked.

"Yeah," W said. "Haven't lived here in awhile. Folks are in Texas."

"Wait," Rechsler said. "Are you...?"

Bush cut him off. "Yeah, that's my grandfather."

"Holy shit," Rechsler said. "A United States senator."

"Man, somethin' smells good," W said. He cut off the small talk. "Wow, looks like meat loaf. Hot dog!" Bush took a seat at one of the long tables. He sat next to Rechsler.

"Gentlemen," Rechsler said. "I'd like to introduce a guest. George Bush. And he's a VIP. His grandfather is the U.S. senator."

"Was," Bush replied as the men applauded their guest. "Was a senator, 'til last year. Can someone pass me the gravy?"

W's attitude won over the brotherhood. They loved his contrary nature. They roared at the "pass the gravy" line.

W had thrown his jacket over the back of his chair. He reached into one of the pockets. He pulled out a beer. Rosenberg, the guy who had invited W and his roommate to the frat house, walked in the room. He sat down next to Bush.

"Now there's a real frat boy," Rosenberg said as he saw W pull out the beer.

"Hey, nothin' but the best for dyke house," W said. He was laughing. He pulled out the beer from the other pocket. He handed it to Rosenberg. "Here's to ya,'" W said. He clicked his can with the one he'd given Rosenberg.

"Glad to have you here," Rosenberg told him.

"Where's the keg?" W asked. He jammed a forkful of meat loaf in his mouth.

"In the next room," Rosenberg said. "Let's finish up here. I'll show you my room."

"And then we can tap the keg?" W asked.

"Then we can tap the keg," Rosenberg said. "Well, actually it's already tapped."

"Well, screw the tour," W said. "I can see your room later. Right now there's some beer to be drunk."

Chapter VI
Fart Rat

Delta Kappa Epsilon was built for George W. Bush.

If there were ever a fraternity founded for professional towel-snappers such as W, this was it. This house was also in the heart of Yale University.

W began moving in to DKE the week before Labor Day. It was his sophomore year. He pledged the house during his previous semester. He made it to the top of his pledge class. The last keg party of his freshman year sealed his reputation as a party boy.

In the lexicon of college-fraternity life, one can't come with a higher recommendation.

"Hey Bushman," someone yelled. W was carrying a box of crap in to the house. It was that first week in September, 1965.

"Hey, how's it hangin'?" Bush yelled. He didn't even know who had shouted to him.

"Better than yours," said the voice. W now recognized who it was. It was one of the upper classmen at the frat.

"In your dreams, big boy," W yelled back. "You wanna suck it now or later?"

Bush got to the big black wooden door of the white-clapboard mansion. He dropped his box of stuff. He extended his hand to Ben McPherson. McPherson was a junior. W and McPherson had drunk late in to the night during that famous last keg party the year before.

"Well kiss my ass. Look who it is," W said. He grabbed McPherson's right hand in one of those overkill handshakes. "You got anything cold to drink?"

"I got something for you to drink but I don't know how cold it is," McPherson replied. He pointed to his crotch. How else to one-up the Bushman?

"In your dreams, crotchman," Bush guffawed. "Hey, I gotta drop this stuff in my room. Then we'll make a beer run."

"Sounds like a plan, W," McPherson said.

Bush continued moving boxes of stuff in to his room. His was a tiny, one-man room on the right front side of the fraternity house. He had ranked high in his pledge class. That derived from his commitment to knowing how to have a good time at keg parties. So Bush had first pick of rooms. He chose a single room. Either that or have a roommate. He had just dropped his last load of belongings in his room. McPherson came by. "You ready?" McPherson asked.

"Ready? Is the pope Catholic?" W asked. "Let's head out. Hell, maybe we can find some. You know. Head?"

"Whatever," McPherson replied.

They walked from the rear door of the frat. They went to the parking lot. McPherson's black Mustang was parked there.

"Hot shit," W said when he saw the car. He hopped in the passenger side. McPherson got behind the driver's wheel. They drove down to Shimmy's Variety. The store was only a couple of miles away. They could buy beer. The owner would never question their legality. The boys bought a case of Pabst. They headed back to the house. They stashed two six-packs each in their rooms. By the time dinner was being served, they'd already each drunk a six-pack. "Hey, let's head over across the street and see if we can pick up some chicks," W said. Yale was in a neighborhood that had a small school. Woodbridge College had a reputation for supplying co-eds for the Yale undergrads. The women at Woodbridge liked being in the company of the Yale guys. The girls especially liked the frat rats. The frat boys in turn had a plentiful supply of women.

McPherson said he liked the idea of looking for women. "I'm with ya," he told Bush. The two of them were already drunk. They walked across South Wollard Street. They headed to one of the brick mansions. They knew it was a girls' dorm at Woodbridge. They were reeking of beer. They walked in the front door. A kindly, elderly woman served as the house mother. She saw the Bush and McPherson enter.

"Hello boys," the grandmotherly woman said. "Can I help you?"

"We're supposed to meet some girls here for a party," W said. He made up the story on the spot.

"Oh, OK," the woman said. "Give me their names, boys. I'll call them down from their rooms."

"Uh, yeah, uh, hey Ben, what's those girls' names again?" W asked McPherson.

"Franny Farkle and Debbie Doolittle," McPherson told him. He made up the names because the boys had no specifics to offer in terms of girls. They just wanted any girl they could get their hands on.

"Right," W said. He had trouble containing his laughter. "Franny Farkle and Debbie Doolittle."

"Jee, um, those names don't ring a bell," the woman told Bush.

"What's your name then?" Bush asked the woman.

"Margaret Daley," she replied.

"You busy tonight?" W asked.

"What?" the elderly Daley asked. "What are you doing to me?"

"Nothing - yet," W replied. He laughed hysterically. "No, ma'am, the thing is, I can't remember who we were supposed to meet."

W. was trying to extricate himself from this mess. An attractive girl walked by.

"Hey," Bush said to her, "we're from DKE. Tryin' to get a little party together, me and Ben here."

"Wonderful," the girl said. "I'm Sara. Sara Conant."

"I'm horny," W said.

Daley looked perplexed. She had no idea what was going on. Conant looked amused. McPherson didn't know what to say or do. Bush was in his element. He liked being a drunken wise guy. He came across as friendly. He was also drunk. He didn't care what he said.

"Lemme see if I can get some more girls," Conant said. She ran up a circular staircase in the old brick house. Bush and McPherson made small talk with the old lady.

A few minutes passed. Conant came bounding down the stairs. "Hey, I found someone!" she said excitedly. "This is Marsha Mahoney."

"Hey Marsha," W said. He extended his right hand. "I'm here to escort you to the balls. I mean the ball. Bush. George W. Bush."

Mahoney had a penchant for drink and men. She put on her innocent, what-do-you-mean look. "So, I hear you guys are having a party?" Mahoney asked. "At DKE?"

"Dyke," W said. "But yeah, come on, let's go."

"Sara, what the hell, let's do it," Mahoney said to Conant.

"OK," Conant said. "Lemme grab a sweater in my room. You want me to bring you down anything?"

"I guess I'm all set," Mahoney said.

"She's set alright," W said, He grabbed her arm. "She's got a nice set."

"God you're awful," she pretended. "Any more like you at home?"

Conant fetched her sweater. She came down the stairs. "OK guys, here we go," she said. "Mrs. Daley, we'll be home late. Don't wait up."

"OK honey," Daley said. "You be good girls. Nice to meet you, boys."

The four of them walked out the front door. They headed down the blue-slate sidewalk toward DKE. W pulled a beer from his pocket. He popped the top. He took a huge mouthful. He handed the can to Mahoney. "Have a swig," he said.

"You hot shit," Mahoney said. She took the beer. She took a big gulp. She swallowed like an old pro.

"That went down fast," W said to her.

"Lots of practice," Mahoney replied. She grinned devilishly. She hit him playfully on the left shoulder.

The four of them got to the frat. Bush suggested they go to McPherson's room. It was much bigger than his. McPherson had two roommates. The room had three beds. "Yeah, great idea," McPherson said. "W, why don't you run by your room? Grab your beer. Bring it upstairs."

"Will do, boy," W replied. "Hey, Mahoney, why don't you come with me? Well, you know what I mean."

"Yeah, whatever George," she said. She smiled. She took his arm. "Gimme another swig of that beer."

W and Mahoney walked down the long, meandering first-floor hallway. They passed three brothers' rooms on the way. Most of the boys at DKE were pre-med students. They weren't like George W. Bush. They took their academics seriously. It wasn't unusual to see many of them in their rooms on a Saturday night such as this. They would be studying.

"Hey Carl," Bush said to one of the upper classman. He saw Carl Donnellon. Bush and date for the night walked by Donnellon's open door. Donnellon was a serious student. He didn't understand George Bush's party style.

"Oh, George, hi," Donnellon said. He recognized Bush as a member of the newest pledge class. He got up to greet Bush.

"Carl I'd like you to meet Marsha Mahorney," W said. Mahoney blushed. But she laughed enjoyably.

"Mahoney, you idiot," she corrected Bush. "I swear you've got sex on the brain."

"I'm from Tex-ass and I like sex-ass," W replied.

"See ya guys later," Donnellon said. He shook his head. He returned to his books.

"Here's my hangout," W told Mahoney. He showed her his room. It was no bigger than a closet. The room double bunk bed that one of the upper classmen had built. It was connected to one wall of the room. The bed literally took up half the room. The foot of the lower bunk contained a built-in shelf. W put his music system there.

"Fire up some tunes," W told Mahoney. "I'll grab the beer."

"Aren't we supposed to meet the other guys, upstairs?" Mahoney asked.

"We'll get to it Marsh," he said. "Hey you'll have to come up to Kennebunkport next summer. We got some nice marshes up there. Not as nice as you though."

"Gimme a break," she replied.

"How 'bout a beer instead?" he asked.

"Deal," she said.

W handed her a beer from the small refrigerator. The frig took up just about all of the available floor space in Bush's tiny room. He also grabbed one for himself. He sat down on the edge of the lower bunk. He popped the top on his beer. "Cheerios," he said. He raised his beer to Mahoney's. "Have a seat."

Mahoney sat down to Bush's right. She turned to her right. She turned on the hi-fi. Bush had bought it in Portsmouth, NH. He had been on his way back to school from Kennebunkport the week before. He knew he wanted a music system for his frat room. He figured he'd pick one up in New Hampshire. He avoided the sales tax. New Hampshire also had cheap booze. Bush couldn't miss an opportunity. He'd buy a few bottles on his way to school. He had a routine. He would go to a liquor store. He would find an adult outside. Better yet if the adult looked like he needed a few bucks. Bush would offer the loser a few dollars to make a buy for him.

W and Mahoney quickly downed a couple more beers. They found themselves lying down on the lower bunk. They were listening to music on Bush's eight-track cassette recorder.

Bush reached up over his left shoulder. He shut off the over-head light. The moonlight was shining in a window. Other-wise it was dark. Bush rolled onto his right side. He slowly put his hand under Mahoney's chin. He gently turned her face toward his. Her eyes were closed. He gave her a kiss. She turned a bit onto her left side. She put her right hand around his left shoulder. They pulled each other closer. Bush slid his hand around Mahoney's back. He slipped her blouse up from her skirt's waistband. He felt the elastic rim of her black tights. He slid his hand slowly up her back. Eventually he reached her bra strap.

"Wow, it's already midnight," W said, waking up a few hours later. Lying beside him was a virtual stranger named Marsha Mahoney. She was a girl from Woodbridge College. Bush had just met her a few hours earlier. The two of them were under the down comforter on the lower bunk of W's bed. He leaned over to his right. He put his lips on Mahoney's. He kissed her.

"Oh," she said. She opened her eyes. "What, wh-, oh, shit, I get it. Man, we must have fallen asleep." She put her arms around him. She pulled him close. "You were wonderful," she told him. "Wow. Only one question. What's your name again?"

"Screw off Mahorney," Bush said.

"I already did!" Mahoney replied. "Hmmmmmmm."

"You weren't so bad yourself," W told her. "How ' bout a beer?"

"That would hit the spot?" she said.

"What spot?" he asked.

"Eat me," Mahoney replied. "Just gimme a damn beer."

"OK Mahorney," W said. He got up. He slipped on his chi-nos. "Coming!"

Bush fetched his bedmate a beer from his refrigerator. He helped himself to one while he was up. "Here ya go," he said. He handed Mahoney a cold can of beer.

"That tastes so good," she said. "Best thing I've tasted to-night."

"You sure?" he asked?

"You're such a wiseass," she told Bush. "Hey, I think I'll blow this joint. I'm gonna head back to the dorm."

"Blow what?" Bush asked.

Mahoney pulled herself up from the bed. She grabbed her underwear, skirt and blouse. She dressed in the dark, moonlight-lighted room. W sat on the edge of the bunk. He sipped his beer.

"Wanna walk me back?" Mahoney asked him.

"Shit, yeah, I guess so," W said. Finish your beer first."

"I'll just take it with me," she replied. She got up. She slipped on her sweater. "Come," she said. She took Bush's hand.

"I already did," he said.

"Gimme a break," she replied. "Let's go."

W and his date left Bush's room. They headed up the hall. They walked out the front door. Into the dark night they ventured. They headed toward Mahoney's dorm. It was just up the street. They got to the door of the dorm. Bush said, "OK Mahorney, I'll catch ya later. That was fun."

"OK George," she said. She gave him a kiss on his left cheek. "Will you tell Sara I left?"

"Left what - your bra in my room?" W asked.

"No, asshole," she said. "Forget it. Forget I asked. I'll talk to you later."

"I'll let Sara know you left - your bra in my room," W said. He tried to be nice. But he caught himself. He had to be a wise guy.

"OK, George. Later," Mahoney said.

Bush headed back to the frat. He pulled his half-drunk beer from his pocket. He tipped it to his mouth. He walked up to the front door of DKE. McPherson and Conant were walking out.

"Hey guys," W said. "Sara, just walked Mahorney back to the dorm. She's not so Mahorney now."

"Whatever," Conant replied. She turned her eyes downward.

"I'll see ya in a few minutes," McPherson told Bush.

McPherson walked Conant back to her dorm. He returned to the frat. He headed down the hall to W's room. "Them chicks weren't half bad, huh?" W said to McPherson.

"Not bad at all," McPherson said.

"Hey," W said. He took another swig of beer. "Is it supposed to snow tonight?" He figured McPherson might understand the inference.

"Snow?" McPherson asked.

"Just kidding," Bush said. "Hey where can we get some weed?"

"Let's check with Jimbo," McPherson said. He referred to one of the upper classmen. They walked down the hall. They knocked on the white paneled door of the house pusher - Jimbo.

The door opened. A strong odor of pot blew out the door. "Hey fellas, come on in," Jimbo said. He introduced another upper classman, Fred Pitt. Pitt was sucking on a joint.

"Quick, take a hit," Pitt said. He handed the joint to W.

Bush sucked hard. He took in a big mouthful of smoke. He held his breath.

"Hold your hit," Pitt told him. "Don't breathe." W finally couldn't hold his breath any longer. He exhaled. He saw stars. "Holy lobster pot," he said. "That stuff is unbelievable. Gimme another hit."

"Give your buddy a hit, too," Jimbo said. He handed the joint to Bush after taking a hit himself.

Bush was now not only feeling the effects of the beers. Now he was high. He collapsed into an overstuffed chair in Jimbo's room. "Fuck me alive," he muttered, closing his eyes. "Man that shit is good."

Jimbo put on some music. Within a few minutes Bush was fast asleep.

"Get up, we've got places to go, people to see," Jimbo said to Bush. Bush was sleeping in Jimbo's chair.

"What the hell time is it Jimbo?" W asked.

"2:15," Jimbo replied.

"I gotta hit the sack," W said.

"No, let's take a ride up to campus," Jimbo replied. "We'll go in my car." Jimbo had a yellow Chevrolet Impala convertible. It had a black rag top. W thought this car was the cat's meow.

"OK," W said. "Just lemme get another beer. Want one?"

"Of course I want one," Jimbo said. He threw on his suede fringe riding jacket. "I'll meet you in the parking lot."

W grabbed a couple of beers. He met Jimbo in the frat's rear parking lot. They hopped in the Impala. They headed to campus.

"Hey let's go up by the gym," W said. "They're doing some construction work up there. Maybe we can grab some good stuff."

"You're high," Jimbo said to him.

"High?" W asked. "There's only one thing higher - the Empire State Building."

"Not bad," Jimbo said.

"Not good, either," W replied. "That's bad weed."

They got to the upper side of campus. They found the construction site W was referring to. "Hey, go over there," he told Jimbo. A huge security floodlight illuminated the area, Bush saw a pile of materials. "Holy shit, look at this," he told Jimbo. "It's glass, frosted glass. We can use some of this. Stop here."

They got out of the car. They inspected the pile of construction materials. "Shit this is good glass," Jimbo said.

"I know," W replied. "That's what I'm here for. Let's see if we can get a sheet of this into the car." They began gingerly lifting a large 2-foot-by-4-foot piece of glass. They moved slowly toward the car. "Open the windows on this side," W told Jimbo. Jimbo opened the driver's door window and the rear window behind it. They began sliding the glass into the car.

"Shit, a security guard," Jimbo said suddenly. He saw a campus police car coming toward them.

"Fuck," W said. "We're fucked."

It was too late to try to return the glass to the pile. They tried to jam it in to the rear seat of the car. W was nearest the driver's seat. He jumped in behind the wheel. Jimbo got in the passenger side front seat.

"Drive. Get out of here," he told Bush.

"Too late," W replied. The police cruiser was now just yards in front of their car. Bush decided it was too late. He couldn't make a run for it."

"'Mornin' gentlemen," the campus cop said. He got out of his car. The cruiser was now facing theirs. Its headlights were aimed at them. It was now 2:35 a.m.

"Hi," W said.

"Everything alright?" the cop asked.

"Oh yeah," W said.

"What's this?" the cop asked. He saw the glass in the car.

"Oh," W said. "We picked it up at the glass shop earlier today. We were just over at the gym working out. Now we're headed down to our frat. We're using the glass for a renovation project."

"OK, fellas, just checkin'," the cop said. The cop got back in his cruiser. He drove off. W drove off too.

"I can't believe he didn't arrest us," Jimbo said. He marveled also at the story Bush had just concocted on the spot.

"I can't either," Bush said.

The boys got back to the frat. They were amazed they hadn't been arrested for theft. They went to bed.

The next morning came. Bush awoke. He decided he needed to cover his tracks. He theorized that if the construction crews figured out someone stole some glass, they would be contacting campus security. Security might put one and one together. They might backtrack to the night before. He went out behind the frat. He removed the glass from Jimbo's car. He hid it beneath an old junk car. The junker was rotting away in one corner of the parking lot. He jumped in his father's car. He drove down to a glass shop in town.

"I need a piece of window glass about 1 foot wide and 2 feet long," Bush told the clerk at the Pittsburgh Plate Glass shop. The clerk went in the back of the shop. He had a piece of glass cut. He returned to the counter.

"Anything else?" the clerk asked Bush.

"Um, no, guess that's all I need," W said. "Only one question. Can you backdate the sales slip by a day?" He never explained to the clerk his strange request.

"Sure, no problem," the clerk said.

Bush paid for the glass. He left the store. He now had a slip for a piece of glass with the previous day's date. The cops might come to him or Jimbo. But the boys now had a bill of sale. They could use it as proof that they had bought glass. They could show a purchase date before their trip to the construction site. The trip was the one they took in a drunken, drug-crazed state.

"Hey, check this out," W said. He breezed into the rear entrance to Jimbo's room. It was only room in the frat with its own entrance. He walked over to Jimbo. Jimbo was reclining in a light-green upholstered chair. He had a phone to his ear. He was watching TV. Bush handed Jimbo the bill of sale from the glass store.

"I don't get it," Jimbo said.

"There's nothing to get," W explained. "Now we have a bill of sale for the glass."

"Hmmm, very interesting," Jimbo said. He resumed his phone conversation. He took toke on a joint. "Here, have a hit," he told W. He pulled the phone from his ear for a second.

"Don't mind if I do," W said. "Guess I'll have to take a pass on accounting lab. My homework won't be done. Mummsy might have to hire a tutor for me."

"Not if you go to class she won't," Jimbo said.

"Big if, big boy," Bush replied. He handed the joint back to Jimbo.

Bush bought an ounce of pot from Kenny Rackliffe. Rackliffe was another sophomore. He also purchased 100 tablets of pharmaceutical amphetamines from Jimbo. Bush decided to skip a full day of classes. He wanted to get high. He called a girl he'd met in his first year at Yale. He wanted to see if Judy Noble wanted to join him.

"Hey Jude," W said, "wanna get high?"

"It's in the middle of the week," she said. "What are you, high?"

"Yes," W said. "What's the point Jude?"

"If you have to ask the question George you won't - or just don't want to - understand the answer," Noble said.

"O.K., fine," W said. "Anyone else over there wanna blow some weed?" Noble was a member of a sorority. She joined Pi Beta Phi. Bush figured that one of her sorority sisters might want to party with him.

"Dunno, lemme check," Noble said. She put her hand over the receiver. She yelled, "Hey anyone up for partying? My friend at DKE has some pot."

"And some speed," W piped in.

"And some speed," Noble yelled.

"Shit yes," came a reply from one of Noble's sorority sisters. "Lemme talk to him."

"George, I may have found someone for you," Noble said. "I'm gonna put her on. Here she is."

"Hello?" the girl said. She took the phone from Noble.

"Hey, George Bush here. Wanna get high?"

"Sure, there or here?" asked the girl.

"Don't matter to me sis'," W replied. "Might as well come down here."

"OK, I'll be there in 10 minutes," the girl said.

"See ya then," Bush replied.

The girl threw on a jacket. She ran out the door. She walked the four blocks from Pi Phi on Williams Avenue to DKE on South Wollard Street. Fewer than 10 minutes has passed. She walked in the door at DKE. One of the brothers was walking by the front door.

"Can I help you?" Joe Heyer asked. He was a straight-laced academic. He was no Bush fan.

"Yeah, I'm looking for George Bush," the girl said.

"Oh, his room is down that hall. Go all the way to the end," Heyer said. "I think he's studying. Joke!"

The girl headed down the hall. She ended up at a tiny room. The sweetness of pot emanated from the room. She knocked on the door. It opened a second later. "Hey," Bush said.

"Hi, are you George?" the girl asked.

"No I'm high," Bush said.

"Hi. Denise Sears," the girl replied.

"Come on in girl," Bush said. "Shut the door." The room smelled strong from pot. Bush was playing music on his hi-fi. He had on a t-shirt and a pair of jeans. His eyes were blood-shot. They were half-closed. He handed her a lighted joint.

"Hold your hits," he said. "This is unbelievable stuff. Don't waste it."

She took a big drag. Bush opened the refrigerator. He pulled out a beer. He handed it to her.

"Thanks," she said. Her teeth were clenched. She was holding her breath. She didn't want to ruin the effect of the pot. She handed him back the joint. "Where you supposed to be?" W asked Sears. He motioned for her to pull up a chair. The room was too small to contain a chair. The only place to sit was on the edge of the lower bunk bed.

"Psychology," Sears answered.

"Lab?" Bush asked.

"No, lecture," Sears said.

"Here, take another hit," W replied. "Why do they have a fucking lab for psych? Whadda they do, operate on your brain?"

"No, idiot," she said. "I don't know. They just call it lab for some reason."

"Who's the prof - Freud?" W asked. He took a big gulp of beer. He needed to wash down his last hit of pot.

"Uh, no," Sears said. "First of all, Freud is dead. Second of all, Freud was a psychiatrist. He wasn't a psychologist."

"What's the fucking difference?" Bush asked. "They're all into the head right? You know, kinda like I'm into head, Sears-and-Roebuck girl."

"Good, George," Sears said. "Real good. FYI, a psychiatrist is a medical doctor. As in MD. As in Medicinae Doctor. As in the Latin for doctor of medicine. The other is a psychologist. He has a Ph.D. It's Latin. Philosophiae Doctor, or doctor of philosophy."

"Do you charge any extra for this head job, Sears-and-Roebuck girl?" Bush asked.

"Hey, now you'll know the difference between a psychologist and psychiatrist," she said. "Now you tell me something. Where should you be right now?"

"In your pants honey babe," W replied.

"Oh come on," Sears replied. She rolled her eyes.

"I'd like to come on you," Bush said.

"OK," she replied. "Now you can be serious. What class are you missing right now?"

"Joint Rolling 101," he said. He grabbed a pack of rolling papers. He reached under the bed. He pulled out a plastic sandwich bag. It was filled with pot. He pulled a paper from the pack. He spread it out on the cardboard cover of one of his records. He opened the bag. He inserted his right forefinger and thumb. He retrieved a pinch of pot. He placed the pot on the paper. He deftly rolled a joint. He raised the finished product to his lips. He moistened with his tongue the edge of the rolling paper. "Good tongue, huh?" W remarked to Sears.

"Tongue this," she replied. She pointed to her behind.

"I'd like to," he said. "Take a toke on this." He pointed to his crotch.

He grabbed a book of matches from the top of his hi-fi. He lit the joint. He took a big hit. He held his breath. He then passed the lighted joint to Sears. She was sitting to his left on the edge of the bed. Sears took a big hit. She held her breath. She passed the joint back to Bush.

"Good work," he said. "Nice sucking action." Sears burst out laughing. A large puff of smoke came billowing from her mouth.

"Jesus Christ you blew that one alright," W said. "Hold your hits."

"I couldn't," she pleaded. "You made me laugh too hard."

"I'd like to be hard," W replied.

There simply was no stopping that boy. He was a wise-ass from the word go. More aptly, from the letter "A."

Bush and Sears passed the joint back and forth. They also drank their beers. Life was a party for George W. Bush. Anyone who cared to join him was a guest. The time of day or night was immaterial. The two of them fell asleep on the bed.

"Anyone in there?" Bush suddenly woke up. He heard someone at his door.

"Who's there?" he mumbled.

"The police," came the reply.

"Screw off Heyer," W said. He recognized the voice on the other side of his door. It was Joe Heyer. He was a frat brother. He had met Sears when she showed up at the front door of the DKE house to visit Bush a few hours earlier. "You guys gonna join us for dinner?" Heyer asked.

"Shit - yes," W said. "What the hell time is it?"

"5:30," Heyer said.

Bush opened the door. "A.M. or P.M.?" he asked. He was squinting.

"P.M.," Heyer replied.

"Holy shit, did we sleep that long?" W asked. He rubbed his eyes. He looked at Sears lying on his lower bunk.

"Huh?" she asked. She opened her eyes. "Man, I'm so high I can't think. What the fuck? Holy shit," she said. She jumped up. "What time is it?"

"Time for you to join us for dinner," W told her.

"Hey, Joe thanks," W said to Heyer. "We'll catch you at dinner. Whadda we have?"

"Pork chops I think," Heyer said.

"Pork who?" W asked.

"George, see you at dinner," Heyer said. He rolled his eyes. He walked away from the pot-stinking room.

Junior rarely heard from his parents. They were still back in Texas with W's four siblings. In late October of his sophomore year, they called. They wanted to let him know of his father's latest political plans. G.H.W. Bush had already lost a U.S. Senate race. That was the year before. So he was going to consider a try at a U.S. House seat.

"We'll see if this works out a little better than the last one," George H.W. Bush told his son. He'd called him the third week in October 1965. "I think I'll probably decide by Christmas."

W was talking to his father on the frat-house phone. It was located down the hallway from his room. One of his frat brothers, Jeff Shaw, was a prankster as much as Bush was. He walked by. He grabbed W in the crotch.

"Ouch!" W shouted. He was still talking to his father on the phone from Texas. "Shaw you asshole."

"What was that?" George H.W. Bush asked his son.

"Oh nothing, Pop. One of the brothers grabbed my nuts."

"OK, son. You're busy so I'll let you get back to business," Junior's father said. He was disgusted. "Say, George? Your mother wants to know whether you're gonna be coming home for Thanksgiving."

"Not sure, Pops," W replied. "I think I might just stay around here. It'll save me a long plane trip - and money."

"When's the last time we made you pay for your own plane ticket?" his father asked him. "Look, George, I'll let you go. I'm gonna run now. Mom sends her love."

"OK, catch ya later Pop," W said. He hung up the phone. He ran into the frat's living room to see if he could find Shaw and goose him back.

Bush awoke in mid-November. He looked out the window. There was an unusually early snowstorm for New England. It was a Saturday. The weather was treacherous. Brothers usually left the house to study at the school's library. It was on campus. But the weather was bad. They were studying at the house.

The weather wasn't too stormy for W's first-year roommate and old friend, Dan Grant, to stop by the house.

"What's up pardner?" Grant asked. He walked in to Bush's room.

"Whadda ya got?" W asked him.

Grant reached beneath his corduroy sport jacket. He pulled out two record albums. He also pulled out a carton of Camel cigarettes.

"Oh, you've been to the bookstore," W laughed.

"You guessed it," said Grant. His idea of fun was seeing how much loot he could steal from the campus bookstore. Grant pulled a plastic baggie from his sport coat's right pocket. "Got this from Jimbo," Grant said. He referred to the house pusher.

"Holy shit, hash, hot dog," W said.

"You got your pipe?" Grant asked.

"Yeah, right there in the drawer," W said. He pointed to an old desk in his room.

Grant opened the drawer. There was a brass hash pipe. He pulled out the pipe. He shut the bedroom door. He broke a corner off the chunk of hash. He crumbled it into the bowl on the hash pipe. He lighted the pipe. He sucked in a hit. He handed it to Bush.

"Hold your hits," Grant told Bush. W sucked in a big mouthful of smoke. He suddenly began coughing. He was also choking.

"Jesus Christ you're wasting good hash," Grant said to him.

"Kiss my ass," W said. "Whadda ya want me to do, gag to death. The smoke went down the wrong way. He took another hit on the pipe. He held his breath.

W and Grant passed the pipe back a forth a couple of times. Grant asked, "Want more?"

"Hit me again baby," Bush said. His eyes were bloodshot.

Grant put another chunk of hash into the pipe. Bush turned on his hi-fi. It was so loud neither Bush nor Grant could hear each other. They were yelling so they could hear each other.

"Hey, someone's knocking on your door," Grant told Bush.

"So open the fucking thing up," W told him.

Grant opened the door. A fraternity brother was standing there. It was Donald Marks. His arms were folded. He had an annoyed half-grin on his face.

"What's up?" W asked.

"You boys doing drugs?" asked Marks. He wasn't the partying type.

"Drug this," W said. "What's up?"

"Could you please turn down that stereo?" Marks asked. "I'm trying to study."

"Christ, it's Saturday," W replied. "Gimme a break. Study somewhere else."

"So you won't turn it down?" Marks asked.

"No," W said.

"If you don't turn it down I'm going to go downstairs to the electrical-service panel and cut the power to your room," Marks said.

"If you do," W replied, "I will go into your room and cut every wire in sight." He was referring to Marks' vast collection of hi-fi equipment. The audio display went from floor to ceiling.

"So you won't turn down your music?" Marks asked.

"No," Bush said.

"OK," Marks said. He left the room. Bush followed him. . . Marks headed for the basement. Marks got to the electrical-service panel. He started to unscrew the fuse providing power to Bush's room.

"If you do it, I'm going to your room to cut every wire I see," Bush said.

Marks backed down. He went back upstairs.

Bush had been bluffing. He had no plans to damage any of Marks' equipment. But his poker face showed a talent that seemed to serve him well. He acted the part when he needed to manipulate a situation to his advantage.

W and Grant went back to Bush's room. They closed the door. They listened to the loud music. They also smoked another bowl of hash. They drank a couple of beers each. They were having a typical Saturday. For them, it was the same as Sunday, Monday, Tuesday, etc.

"Shit, wonder if we can get on the roof," W suddenly said to Grant.

Grant looked quizzical. But he was interested.

"It would make a great place to fire snowballs down onto the road," W said. He grabbed a jacket. "Follow me," he said to Grant. He ran down the hall. He got to the main stairway. He led Grant up the stairs to the second floor. He went into a large room. It was toward the back of the house.

He had Grant in tow. He walked into the room. Four of the frat brothers lived in the room.

"Hey Willie-boy," W said. He saw Will Winchill. "Didn't you once tell me we could get to the roof from here?"

"Yeah, right there," Winchill said. He pointed up to a trap door in the ceiling. "Just push that open and you're on the roof. Why?"

"'Cause it's snowing out," W replied.

"And?" Winchill asked.

"And I wanna throw snowballs onto the street," W replied.

"You guys are high, aren't you?" Winchill asked. He suddenly figured out the score of the game.

"Who us?" Bush asked. He grabbed a chair. He wanted to stand on the chair to reach the trap door in the ceiling.

Bush got up on the chair and pushed open the trap door. That exposed the roof. He hoisted himself up. "Come on," he told Grant. Heavy snow poured down through the hole.

Grant hoisted himself up. The two boys were now on the slippery roof. The snowstorm had picked up in intensity over the morning. W and Grant were in blizzard conditions on the roof.

W bent down. He grabbed a couple of fistfuls of snow. He began making a snowball. He wound up like a pitcher. He threw it toward Wollard Street. The heavy, wet snowball smashed with a loud bang into the side of a passing car. "Bull's eye!" W yelled excitedly. He slipped as he threw the snowball. He grabbed on to Grant. He nearly fell off the roof to the ground below. "Did you bring the hash?"

"Of course," Grant said. He pulled out the pipe. He pulled out his baggie of hash. He covered the pipe with his jacket. He loaded the bowl with hash. He pulled out his cigarette lighter. He tried to light the pipe. The flame kept going out. Finally, he got it lighted. He took a big hit. He passed it to Bush.

W took a hit. He held his breath. He handed the pipe to Grant. He bent down to make another snowball. He threw it toward the street. It landed in the middle of the road. It narrowly missed a car that had just passed. He made another huge snowball. Again he threw it toward the road. This one landed smack in the middle of a passing car's windshield. There was a big splash. The car suddenly pulled over.

"Holy shit," W said to Grant. "I hit their windshield. Let's get inside - quick."

W shimmied down the opening onto the chair below. Grant followed. He replaced the cover on the trap door.

"Too cold out there for ya?" Winchill asked.

"No, too dangerous," W said. He looked at Grant. He winked. "Willie, got any beer?"

"Shit no, it's the middle of the day," Winchill said. What are you, high?"

"Not high enough," W replied. His comment prompted Winchill to shake his of the head. Winchill laughed. He admired Bush's perspective on life.

It was a week before Thanksgiving. W was still trying to de-cide whether he wanted to fly to his parents' place in Houston for the holiday. He wasn't particularly interested. It would be long flight. He would only be in Texas four days. Then he would have to return to campus for mid-year finals.

Then Christmas would come only a month later. He'd have to decide, again, whether to go back to Texas. The option again would be to just stay at the frat house until the spring semester started in January.

"You gonna go home for Thanksgiving?" W's friend and frat brother, Dan Grant, asked him. They were in the midst of yet another pot-smoking party in Bush's room at the frat house.

"Shit, I dunno," W said. "I wanna fly all the way to Texas about as much as I want my left nut cut off."

"Take a toke on this," Grant said. He handed Bush a joint. "If you want you can come to my parents' for Thanksgiving."

Grant's parents still lived in New Haven. If he went to their house he would avoid a long trip home. He'd also avoid all the baggage, so to speak.

"Not a bad idea," Bush said. He handed the joint back to Grant. "Shit, why not, right?"

"Yeah, hell, why not?" Grant replied. He took another hit. "I'll tell my mother we'll have one more."

"Smoke this," W said. He handed Grant back the joint. "Sounds cool. Guess I better let Mummsy know."

"You gonna call her now?" Grant asked. "What are you, high?"

"Yeah, to both questions," W replied. "Why?"

"'Cause she'll be able to tell you're fucked up," Grant said.

"She already knows," W replied. He picked up the phone to dial home.

"Hello?" Barbara Bush said. She picked up the phone in her kitchen in Houston.

"Hey Mummsy," W replied.

"Georgie, hi, how's it goin'?" his mother asked.

"Cool," he said. "Hey Mummsy, I think I'm gonna stay here for Thanksgiving."

"Why?" she asked. "You're more than welcome here. I know your father would like to see you. And your brothers and sis-ter, of course."

"Well, Dan Grant said I could come to his parents' house," W replied. "You know, Mummsy, they live here in New Haven.

I wouldn't have to fly all the way back for just a few days before I have to come back for finals."

"Well, whatever you wanna do," she said. She was disappointed. "I think your father was hoping you'd be around. He wants to talk to you about his plans to run for that House seat."

"Heck, Mummsy, he doesn't need my advice," W replied. "In fact, he'd probably do better without it."

"You know he values your opinion," Barbara Bush said. "You sound tired."

"Gimme a break, Mummsy," W said. "He values my opinion about as much as he likes to go to the dentist."

"Georgie, I'm surprised at you," his mother said. "What's gotten in to you?"

"Nothing, Mummsy," Junior replied. "The facts are the facts."

"Well, anyway, if you change your mind you're still welcome home," she said.

"OK, thanks Mummsy," W replied. "Guess I'll talk to ya later. Bye."

"Bye honey," she said.

W hung up. He grabbed a beer. He popped the top. "Let's celebrate," he told Grant. "I'm staying here for turkey day."

"Cool," Grant said.

"On one condition." W added, "Your mother will give me the breast."

"What?" Grant asked.

"The breast, you know, from the turkey," W said.

Grant shook his head. He took a swig on his beer. While in New Haven young Bush was having the party of his life. He'd just disappointed his mother again.

Barbara Bush hung up the phone back in Texas. She hung her head. She was pensive in thought. Dorothy was her six-year-old daughter. Dorothy walked in to the kitchen.

"Mommy, I'm hungry," Doro said. "Can I have a peanut-and-jelly sandwich?"

"OK Doro," her mother said. "You know where the stuff is."

"Mommy, why are you sad?" Doro asked.

"Honey, Georgie isn't coming home for Thanksgiving," Barbara Bush said. "Mommy is gonna miss your big brother."

"Oh Mommy, don't worry," Doro said. She placed a chair in front of a cupboard. She got up on the chair to reach the jar of Jiffy peanut butter and Welch's grape jelly. "Mommy can I have some milk?"

"Honey you can get the milk," her mother said. "You know how to do that."

It was two weeks before Christmas. The headmaster at the fraternity was Joel Phelps. He was looking for volunteers to pick out a Christmas tree for the house. He was tacking a sign-up sheet on the back of the front door as Bush was headed to campus. "Hey W, lookin' for help with the tree if you can spare some time," Phelps said. "You'd be good. No one's got spirit like you."

"Shit, consider it done," W said. "I'm headed up to the dean's office. After that I've got a few hours to kill. Any preferences?"

"No," Phelps said. "Something seven, eight feet tall, something like that'll do. We can put it in the living room."

"OK, JP," Bush said. "I'll scope one out later. You'll have it by tonight."

Bush headed out to campus. He would go looking for a tree after a brief stop on campus. He decided to take his father's car. He parked in a "faculty only" lot. The parking spot was next to the administration building. If the worst happened he would get yet another parking ticket. The car was registered to his father. He didn't care whether he got one ticket or a thousand. It would be his father's problem.

Bush had to run in to the dean's office. He had gotten a warning letter in his American history class. History was his major. This wasn't good.

"I got a notice I should check in here," W told a secretary. She was seated just inside the dean's office. "What's your name? Oh, never mind. I see your nameplate. Vickie Walker, eh? Hmmm. I'm a Walker, too. George Walker Bush. You do much walking?"

"Nice to meet you Mr. Bush," Walker said to him. "Did you bring your notice with you?"

"Right here," he said. He handed the woman the warning letter.

"OK," she said. "The assistant dean is handling these matter. He isn't in just now. I will let him know you came in. He will appreciate your concern. He may give you a call. I doubt you'll have to come in again."

"Uh, ma'am," W laughed, "I am not sure that 'concerned' is what I am, but whatever it takes to get that diploma. You live around here?"

"Yes, I do," Walker said.

"Well, you're a good woman," W replied. He smiled "I'll catch ya later."

Bush bounded down the circular marble staircase. The stairs were just outside the dean's office. He went out the front door. He walked around the back of the building to his car. "Figures," Bush muttered. He saw the ticket on his windshield. He grabbed the ticket from under the driver's windshield wiper. He threw it on the ground. He jumped in the car. He headed downtown to a Christmas-tree stand.

W arrived at the stand. He double-parked his car. It was sticking half-way into the narrow street. He went up to the makeshift, outdoor shed. The New Haven Rotary Club was selling trees. "Need somethin' 'bout seven, eight feet," Bush told the attendant.

"Right over there," the attendant said. He pointed to a display near the front of the tree stand. Bush walked over. He pulled out a tree. He looked it up and down. He dragged it over to the shed.

"This'll do," he said.

"She's got nice boughs," the attendant said.

"I've seen better," W said. He smirked. "How much I owe ya'?"

"Five bucks'll do it," the attendant said.

Bush pulled a $5 bill from his pocket. "Here ya' go," he said. "Got some string?"

The attendant gave Bush a roll of twine. He also gave him a knife. Bush tied the tree to the top of his father's car. He returned the roll and knife to the attendant. He left the tree display. The trip back to the frat house took a few minutes. Bush zipped into the lot at the frat house. He sped down the dirt driveway to the rear lot. He parked the car. He pulled the tree inside. He dropped it in the living room.

"Nice job, W," one of the brothers, Peter Howard, told Bush. "There's a tree stand in the closet off the kitchen."

"Stand on this," W said. He pointed to his crotch. "OK, OK, I'll get the stand." He fetched the stand. He raised the tree.

A few hours passed. Several brothers took out a massive entanglement of strings of Christmas lights. They strung them on the tree.

Night fell. W decided to get in the Christmas spirit. He rolled a joint. He opened a beer. He sat down in the living room. The room was dark except for the tree's lights. It got later. Bush decided to light the joint. By about 2:30 a.m. he was high. He was also tired. He lay down on the brown vinyl sofa. He fell fast asleep.

He got up the next morning. W decided that he'd had such a peaceful night with the tree. It was quiet. He liked the solitude. He would stay at the house over the Christmas holiday. The hell with flying back to Texas. He'd rather stay at school. He would get high. He'd have the frat to himself.

Several days passed. It was three days before Christmas Eve. Bush called his mother. "Mummsy, I'm gonna stay here for Christmas. Probably have dinner with the Grants again."

"Oh," his mother said from Houston. "I just don't know Georgie. Do what you want. Goodbye."

W felt bad. He hurt his mother. He didn't want to fly to Texas for Christmas. It was the day before Christmas. The frat house was virtually empty. Bush called Dan Grant. "Hey, no one's around. Come on by and we'll get high in front of the Christmas tree," W told Grant.

"I'm on my way," Grant said. "I've got some more hash." Grant arrived at the house a few minutes later. W was in the living room. He was drinking beer. "Light up that pipe baby," he told Grant. "Let's get it on."

Grant lighted the hash pipe. He took a good hi. He gave it to W. Bush took a big hit.

A few minutes had passed since they began smoking. "Holy shit," he said. "You have a knack for finding good stuff. Beer in my refrigerator if you want one."

Grant went to fetch a beer. The two sat on the floor by the tree. They smoked more hash. They drank more beer. The sun came up the next morning. Bush and Grant awoke. They'd fallen asleep on the couches. They were in the living room.

"Man oh man, we sure crashed, eh Danny?" Bush said.

"Holy shit, I'm wiped," Grant said. "Let's get some breakfast."

They left the house. They headed downtown. They went to a local diner. They both had scrambled eggs, bacon and hash browns. They also had orange juice and coffee.

"I'm stuffed," Grant said.

"I'm George," W replied. "Let's head back."

They got back to the house. They walked in the front door. They smelled something burning.

"What the fuck?" W asked. He figured out the smoke was coming from the living room. "Holy shit, get some water," he told Grant. Bush had found a t-shirt under the Christmas tree. It was smoldering and near flames.

Grant rushed in with a cup of water from the bathroom. He poured it on the burning shirt.

"I think we musta dropped some ashes when we were getting high last night," W said to Grant. "We're lucky the whole frat didn't burn down."

Chapter VII
Bachelor of Farts

It was 1968. George W. Bush was a senior at Yale. The party was almost over. He'd soon have to make a Hobson's choice. Would he go out and find a job? Would he enlist in the military?

The prospect of either sounded daunting. The eldest of former U.S. Sen. Prescott Bush's grandchildren was scared. He had a simple life. He partied. His undergrad years were fun. W was also the eldest of U.S. Rep. George H.W. Bush's children. The senior Bush had been elected two years earlier. He represented Texas' Seventh District in the nation's capital.

The Vietnam War was raging. The political division in the U.S. over the nation's involvement was worsening. More and more American soldiers were dying. A growing number of Americans saw a useless cause. Young George W. Bush was trying to find a way to dodge the bullet. Either go to war or go to work. He was afraid of both options.

It was now mid-march, 1968. Bush was suffering a wrenching hangover. He woke up on a Saturday morning. He was living in a small house. He was renting it with two other Yale students. He sat up in bed. He put his feet on the cold oak floor. He held his head in his hands. His head throbbed. His roommate's stereo was blaring.

"Turn that fucking thing down," W yelled to Randall Howe. Howe was a junior. His room was located just across a small foyer from Bush's.

"Eat shit," Howe yelled back. "Hell, it's 11 fucking o'clock, man. 'Bout time you got your ass out of bed anyway."

Bush rubbed his eyes. He tried to rid himself of the shakes. He was drinking regularly. Waking up drunk or with a hangover was routine.

Bush heard his roommate playing some music. It sent chills up his spine. It was an album by Barry Sadler. Sadler was an ex-Greet Beret. Sadler had begun singing about the war. He had returned from combat in Vietnam.

George W. Bush had been trying to put off the inevitable. He couldn't decide what to do when he would finish school in

May 1968. His drinking was already bad enough. It grew even more frequent as his senior year wore on. He was now nearing the end of his spring semester. The end was near. Partytime was almost over.

"Hey hippie-boy, we got any beer in this house?" W asked Howe. Howe's long hair had earned him the honor of a nickname from Bush.

"Should be some in the refrigerator," Howe yelled back. "Wait, you haven't even had breakfast yet. What are you, high?"

"I wish," W said. "I wish." He slowly lifted himself from the edge of his bed. He threw on a t-shirt and jeans. He went into the tiny bathroom. It was just outside his bedroom. He turned on the cold water. He cupped his hands under the spigot. He collected some water. He lifted it to his face. He did this several times. He tried to wash away the throbbing in his head. Bush grabbed a towel. He wiped his face. He walked down the stairs. He got to the first floor of the house. He entered the kitchen. He opened the white refrigerator. He peered in to see if he could find some beer. Toward the rear of the second shelf were two cans of Miller. He reached for one and took it out. He popped the top. He took a big gulp. He swallowed loudly.

"Man, that hits the spot," he said to no one in particular.

"What's that?" Howe yelled down from his bedroom.

"Nothing," W said. "But since you asked, hippie-boy, what do you think I should do?"

"Do about what?" Howe asked.

"About the fucking draft," Bush replied.

"What - what are you talking about George?" Howe said to him.

"Come on down and talk to me," W said. "I can't compete with your fucking stereo."

A few minutes passed. Howe shut off his stereo. He came down the stairs. He found Bush sitting at the table in the dining room. W was pensively pondering his beer. Bush had the can on the table in front of him. His hands were wrapped around it. He seemed despondent. He was not the usual happy-go-luck George W. Bush.

"What's up W?" Howe asked. He put his hand on Bush's left shoulder. "You don't seem yourself."

"Grab a beer Howe," W said. "I want your opinion on something."

"How 'bout I make some coffee?" Howe replied. "I'm not ready for a beer this morning."

"OK," W said. "Whatever."

Howe put some water in a metal tea kettle. He put it on the stove. He put a spoonful of instant Nescafe in a cup. He poured some hot water over the coffee. He returned the kettle to the stove. He turned off the burner. He put some milk in his coffee. He walked in to the dining room. He sat down next to Bush. "So tell me what's on your mind," Howe said.

"Lots," W replied. "I need to decide what to do."

"Whadda ya mean?" Howe asked.

"Well, if I don't go to grad school, I'm gonna be drafted, for sure, unless the war ends, and if that happens I'm gonna have to get a damn job," Bush replied.

"Jesus, George," Howe said, shaking his head. "Wait, let's think this through. Hold on - what are you worried about?"

"Whadda ya' mean?" Bush wondered. He looked at Howe. "Christ George, your father. He must be able to help you somehow. Have you asked him?"

"Nah," W replied. "I don't talk to him that much. Sorta afraid of asking him to grease the skids for me."

"And your grandfather," Howe added. "Shit, George, you've got it made. Your grampa, a former senator? Your father in Congress. Holy cow, I don't think you've really got so much to worry about."

To Bush, the prospect of getting his father, or grandfather, or both, involved in helping him avoid the draft seemed interesting. But he was reluctant to ask them for the favor. He needed to find a way out of the draft. He might otherwise go to Vietnam. That idea alone made the thought of having to get a job or going to grad school seem tame. Bush pondered Howe's idea. It made more sense to him as time went on.

The senior Bush three months before - in January 1968 - had just returned from what he called a congressional "fact-finding" trip to Vietnam. The U.S. was waging a war. The elder Bush said it was "tearing the country apart." The senior Bush told friends he was following the war "with a great deal more interest now." He claimed it was because he had seen the country of Vietnam itself. He made no mention of what was really on his mind. He was wondering privately whether his eldest son would be drafted to war.

Congressman Bush had moved his family to Washington shortly after his election to the U.S. House. That was in November 1966.

Two years later his eldest son drank a beer on a Saturday morning, in March 1968. He decided to call his father. The senior Bush was in the nation's capital.

W finished his beer. He walked in to the kitchen. He tossed his empty in to the wastebasket. He went to the refrigerator. He grabbed the last Miller. "I'm gonna do the dirty deed," he told Howe. Howe was sitting in the living room studying.

"Whadda ya' mean?" Howe asked.

"Gonna call pop," W said. He walked from the kitchen. He ended up in the living room. He had a cold beer in his hand.

"Hell, I say, why not?" Howe replied. "Shit, that's what I would do if I were you."

"If you were me, you'd be trying to decide whether to run down to Shimmy's Variety right now to pick up some more beer or call your father first," W replied. "Wanna run down to Shimmy's with me?"

"No, George," Howe said. He laughed. "Call your father. Maybe we can make a beer run after that."

"OK, hippie-boy," W said. "If you insist."

W took the green phone from a shelf. It was beside the mantle over the fireplace. It was in the living room. He dragged it over to an easy chair in the middle of the room.

"Here goes nothin'," he said to Howe. He dialed his parents' house in Washington, DC. The phone rang three times.

"Hello?" Barbara Bush said. She picked up the receiver in her kitchen.

"Hey Mummsy," W said.

"Hi Georgie," his mother replied. "What's new?"

"Ah, not too much," W said. "Just thought I might ask Pops somethin'."

"Oh, OK honey, just a second," she said.

W heard his mother calling his father to the phone. "George, it's Georgie - he wants to talk to you," W heard his mother say.

"He's coming," Barbara Bush told W. "Just a second."

"Hello there," George H.W. Bush said into the phone.

"Hello, Congressman," his son said. He laughed.

"What's up kid?" the elder Bush asked.

"Not much, dad," W replied. "I was just wondering somethin.' I can't decide what I should do with school ending. What do you think?"

"Well, son," the elder Bush said. "If you don't go to grad school you're gonna get nailed by the draft."

"That's what I was afraid you might say," W replied. "I had another idea."

"What's that?" his father asked.

"Well," W said, "any chance you could pull some strings for me?"

"How so?" his father asked.

"The Guard," W said. "If you could pull some strings to get me in to the Air Guard it might save my ass."

"Oh, I see," Congressman Bush replied. "Hmmm, it's a thought. Let me think about that - . Heck, why not. If I do it, you've gotta promise me you won't screw off. If we pull this off, and you can't go AWOL. We'll be in a mess. As long as you understand that, OK. I'll see what I can do."

"Oh, yeah, no problem," W said. "Wow, if you can pull this off I'll do what I need to."

"OK, son," the senior Bush said. "I'll let you know what I find out."

"OK, pops, thanks," W said. "Talk to ya' later." He hung up the phone. He punched the air with his fist. He took a big swig of beer.

"OK, Howe, now can we make a beer run?" W asked his roommate. Howe was sitting nearby. He heard W's end of the conversation.

"Yeah, whatever," Howe said. "What did your father say? You think he can help you?"

"I guess so," W said. "He said he'd see what he can do. He told me if I screw up, there'll be hell to pay. Whose car you wanna take, yours or mine?"

"Don't matter, W," Howe said. "Lemme grab some money."

"No prob," W said. "It's on me this time. I owe you. Hell, I might not have called if it hadn't been for you, hippie-boy."

W and Howe prepared for their beer run.

W's father was down in Washington. The first-term congressman - and son of a former U.S. senator - was thinking about making the first overtures to save his son's ass.

"I'm gonna make some calls," the senior Bush said to his wife.

"Oh, OK," Barbara Bush said. She relaxed with a cup of coffee. She was in her kitchen. "What's going on?"

"George wants me to see if I can get him into the Guard," the elder Bush told his wife. He stood by the kitchen sink. The window view overlooked the nation's capital. The cherry blossoms were starting to bud. This wouldn't be the first time the Bush family took advantage of their privilege to avoid military service.

In 1916 there were uprisings in Mexico and along that country's border with the United States. The president of Yale at the time intervened with the U.S. War Department. He persuaded officials there to let Yale undergrads who were members of the Connecticut National Guard to return to school before they saw potential combat. Prescott Bush, father of George H.W. Bush was among them.

George H.W. Bush hoped to advance his own political career. He was afraid. The public couldn't find out he was trying to arrange a cozy deal for his son. He wanted to keep his kid out of Vietnam. The effort could prevent his ever climbing the political ladder. He might not make it to the U.S. Senate. He might not make it beyond the U.S. House.

"I hope no one gets wind of this," he told his wife.

"Well, I suppose it could come out in the press," his wife told him. "I shudder at the thought of Georgie going to Vietnam. I just don't know. If he doesn't go on to grad school, he's gonna get drafted."

"Yeah, OK," George H.W. Bush replied. "I would never forgive myself. He can't go to Vietnam."

George W. Bush's father picked up the phone. He dialed his chief of staff. His chief of staff was Bruce Choate.

"Hello?" Choate said, picking up the phone.

"Brucie," the senior Bush said.

"Oh, congressman, hi," Choate said, recognizing his boss' voice. "This must be important."

"Well, yeah, I guess it is," Bush replied. "I hate to bother you on the weekend but - "

"Don't mention it, sir," Choate said. "How can I help?"

"Oh, Bruce, you're so kind," Congressman Bush said. "I'm worried about something. I'm wondering what to do."

"What's the matter, sir?" Choate asked. "It's Georgie," his father replied. "He - "

"Is he OK," Choate asked. He interrupted his boss.

"Well, yeah, he's OK," Bush's father said. "But I'm worried about the draft, Bruce. You know, he'll be finishing school in May and - "

"The draft," Choate said.

"Right," the congressman answered. "You never miss a beat, do you Brucie?"

"Well, thanks congressman," Choate said. "But it's a big deal. Ya' know, I was wondering what your son planned to do when he finishes school. I didn't wanna pry, ya' know? And so I didn't ask. I guess I should have."

"No, no," the elder Bush said. "For heaven's sake. I just figured I'd give you a call. It was on my mind. I wanted to see what you think. Georgie had called this morning. He wondered whether I could do something. He wants to get this monkey off his back. Do you think we could contact someone? I dunno. Maybe someone at the Texas Air National Guard?"

"Absolutely," Choate said. "Lemme think a second... Listen, why don't I plan on making some calls when I get to the office on Monday. We'll take it from there."

"OK," the elder Bush said. "That would be great Bruce. Really 'preciate it."

"My pleasure congressman," Choate replied. "We'll get going on this first thing. I really don't think this is going to be a problem."

"You don't?" Bush asked.

"No, sir," Choate replied. "You've gotta remember, sir, you are an elected member of the U.S. Congress. You set the Pentagon's budget. Those guys don't like to pick fights with congressmen. Fact they go out of their way just to avoid problems that could screw up their budget."

"Yeah, I guess that's right," Bush said. "I always feel better after talking to you."

"No problem, sir, you enjoy the rest of your weekend and we'll be on this first thing next week," Choate said.

"OK, Bruce, thanks so much," Bush said. "I'll see ya' Monday."

"OK, congressman, if you have any concerns you call me, even if it's before then," Choate said. "Thanks again Bruce," Bush said. "See ya."

Bush hung up the phone. He sat in silence. He pondered what he had just done. He seemed more worried about inappropriately pulling rank. Why wasn't he so concerned whether his eldest child would end up getting drafted? He could go to war and be killed. He decided he had no option.

"I called Bruce," Bush yelled to his wife. "He's gonna make some calls Monday."

"Oh, you talked to him," Barbara Bush said. She walked into the den. Her husband was sitting at his desk. "What did he say?"

"I just told you," her husband replied. He was testy. "He said he'd call some people Monday to see what can be done."

"You don't have to get snippy," she replied. "For crying out loud."

"OK, OK," her husband said.

Barbara Bush walked out of the den. She dropped the subject. She began cleaning the kitchen. Her husband got up from his chair.

"I'm heading over to the club," he said. "I'll be back in a couple of hours."

His wife didn't respond.

Choate arrived at the capitol the following Monday morning. He walked in to his office. He put his brief case on a chair next to his desk. He picked up the phone. He checked his messages.

"Hi Bruce," said the first message. "George here. If the Guard puts up a fuss, let 'em know I'll be glad to meet with them. See ya' Monday."

The message was from Choate's boss. U.S. Rep. George H.W. Bush had left it. It had been left on his phone. It came in at 2:37 p.m. Saturday, according to the time stamp. The message came shortly after Choate had talked to Bush on the phone that morning.

Choate may not have appreciated the importance that his boss was placing on this assignment. Its priority was underscored. Choate would have attended to the task whether or not his boss had left him a phone message. Choate got the point nonetheless. This was a big deal to the Bush family. W's father saw it as such.

Choate listened to his boss' message on his phone. He hung up the receiver. He sat down at his desk. He opened the right bottom file drawer. He pulled out the folder marked "Pentagon - Contacts." He ran down the list of name. He settled on Timothy Hughes. Hughes was the Texas congressional delegation's Pentagon liaison. He dialed Hughes' number. A few seconds passed. A woman answered the phone in Hughes' office.

"Hello, it's Bruce Choate in Congressman Bush's office," Choate said when the woman answered.

"Good morning, Mr. Choate, it's Pam Halley. I am Lt. Hughes' assistant. How are you?"

"Fine thanks Ms. Halley, and you?" Choate replied.

"I am well thank you, Mr. Choate," Halley replied.

"Would you like to speak to Lt. Hughes?"

"I would appreciate it, yes," Choate responded.

"He's right here," Halley said. "I would be glad to put you through." She put Choate momentarily on hold.

Hughes picked up his phone. "Hi, Bruce, it's Tim Hughes, how are you?" Hughes said.

"Fine thank you and you sir?" Choate replied.

"Good thanks," Hughes said. "What may I do for you this morning?"

"Thanks lieutenant for asking," Choate said. "I am calling for Congressman George Bush."

"Why of course," Hughes said. "The gentleman from the Seventh District."

"Yes," Choate said. He laughed. "He's asked me to check with your agency about openings in the Texas Air Guard this spring."

"Oh, sure," Hughes replied. "I'd be glad to check on that. I do know they are being very selective. Well, you know, a lot of folks are hoping to get in the guard now."

"Yeah, I figured," Choate said. "But this isn't anybody."

"Oh?" Hughes said.

"Yeah, lieutenant, it's Congressman Bush's son, George W. Bush. He's finishing school - Yale - this May. He needs to figure out what he's going to do after that."

"Sure," Hughes said. "Let's see what we can do. I'll make some checks. I'll give you an update this afternoon on where we stand. How does that sound?"

"That would be wonderful, lieutenant," Choate replied.

"I can't thank you enough."

"My pleasure, Bruce," Hughes said. "I'll give you a call later today."

"OK, excellent, talk to you then lieutenant," Choate said. "Bye now."

Choate hung up the phone. He hoped he would have some news for his boss later in the day. Hopefully it would be sooner. He felt very awkward calling the Pentagon. He didn't like asking for such favors. He believed that political privilege shouldn't be used for advantage. He received requests daily from constituents. They were all looking for alternative service. They didn't want their sons to die in Vietnam. Why should Bush pull rank? Why should wealth save his ass? Was his life more precious than a kid who was poor? Choate didn't think so.

Choate realized the realities of political life. He was in the capital of the world's most powerful country. A congressman tasked his chief of staff with an assignment. The unspoken rule was perform. The alternative was losing your job.

Congressman Bush arrived on capital hill mid-morning that Monday. He bounded quickly up the capital stairs. He headed for his office. He walked in to the office. He walked through a short hallway. He arrived in to his personal office. He dropped the briefcase he was carrying on a leather chair. It was next to his cherry antique desk. He threw his trench coat over the back of the same chair. He got behind his desk. He was still standing. He unbuttoned his right-sleeve shirt cuff. He unbuttoned the left cuff. He looked quickly at a briefing paper on his desk. Choate had prepared it the previous Friday. He walked across the hall. He entered Choate's office.

"Hi Bruce," the congressman said.

"Hello, sir," Choate said.

"How are we doin' today?" Bush asked. Choate knew he was under the gun. His boss wanted answers. Bush wanted to get his son out of the crosshairs of the Selective Service Commission in Houston. Bush hadn't yet mentioned the issue this Monday morning. Choate broached the topic. His training required it.

"Sir," he said to Bush. "I talked this morning with Tim Hughes, a - "

Bush cut him off. "Oh, sure, over at the Pentagon."

"Right, sir," Choate said. "Anyway, I explained to him we are interested in looking at options for your son, George. I told him that if possible we'd like to see if there is a slot available in the Texas Air Guard."

"Right," Bush said. "What did he say?"

"He said he'd start making checks ASAP," Choate said. "He said he would give me an update on his progress later today."

"OK, sounds good Bruce," Bush replied. "It's a tough one. Junior shudda thought about this earlier. Well, maybe I should have thought about it earlier. But you know. I was hoping the issue would just go away. I guess I was doing some wishful thinking. I didn't wanna admit that the war could last this long. I didn't want to think that my kid could end up in combat."

Choate told his boss that he understood his concerns. He said he would keep him posted on the Pentagon's researching options for W. "Don't worry, sir," he told Bush. He got up from behind his desk. He put his hand on Bush's right shoulder. "We'll work something out."

The congressman nodded. He looked down. He was silent. He walked out of Choate's office. He looked downtrodden.

George W. Bush was biding his time at Yale. He'd be done at school in just eight weeks. All he had to do was hold his own in terms of his grades. He knew he needed to do adequately on his finals. He needed to maintain a high-enough grade point average. He might need a military deferment to go to grad school.

W's last class on Mondays during his spring semester at Yale was an advanced economics lab. It was a discussion period. Students and their professor would simply talk back and forth. They would posit and test various economic theories. Professors often invited guest lecturers to such sessions.

Bush walked in to the lab. A few students were milling about. They waiting for the class to begin.

"Hello Mr. Bush," said the professor, Malcolm Bayer.

"Hey," W said.

"And how is Mr. Bush today?" Bayer asked.

"I'll be better once I can get a cold beer in to me," he said. He laughed. "So let's get this show on the road."

"You're a hard charger, Bush," Bayer said. "You must be trying to outdo your grandfather, huh?"

"What's that supposed to mean?" W asked.

"Oh, George, I was just kidding," Bayer said. "I know your grampa was a U.S. senator. I figured I'd try to get you going. And anyway, competition is a great motivator. If you can outdo your grandfather, hell, you never know. There are no limits to ambition in this country. In fact, maybe we should make that our topic today. Ambition relates to capitalism's economic engine."

"Please, let's not," W said. "Not sure I wanna get in to my family life in class. I mean, would you?"

"Would I what, George," Bayer asked.

"Would you wanna get in to your family life," Bush replied.

"Oh, hell, why not," Bayer said. "But mine's not necessarily as interesting as yours. My grandfather wasn't a U.S. senator. He was a cobbler."

"Oh, all the better," W said. "OK, how about we discuss both our grandfathers. Let's talk about how they shaped our respective life's missions. Did they help us? Did they hurt? Were they a wash?"

"Holy cow, I am quite impressed, young man," Bayer said. "Let's do it."

"Don't young-man me," W said. "I could start my Bayer aspirin jokes if you want."

"No, no, spare me, George, I've heard 'em all," Bayer replied.

Bush took a seat in the class.

"OK, folks, let's start," Bayer said. He addressed the students still milling about the room. The remaining students took seats. Their professor started the discussion.

"Mr. Bush here has an idea for our topic today," Bayer said. "Grandparents - how they motivate us. Did I get it right George?"

"Dunno," W replied. He smirked. "Since it was your idea, maybe you know better than me."

"Ah, Mr. Bush is too modest," Bayer told the class. "He truly is the one who came up with our topic today."

The class for the next hour tossed back and forth ideas and theories. They wondered how a preceding generation can influence those who come in its wake. George W. Bush found himself in the spotlight during the debate. He had been credited with proposing the topic. He was also the grandson of a former U.S. senator. He was the son of a current U.S. congressman.

After class Bush left the lecture hall. Bayer approached him. "Good job, kid," the professor said. He knew his terminology would get under Bush's skin. He couldn't resist. W was a challenge.

"Hey, don't 'kid' me," W replied. He smiled. "Hey Bayer, I'll catch ya later - if I have a headache. Yuck, yuck."

"Yeah, yuck, yuck, is right, Junior," Bayer replied.

"OK, you win," W said. "I'm off to the package store."

W left Metzler Hall. He headed for his apartment. He walked down Oak Street. It connected Wollard Street to the main campus. The house Bush rented was on Locust Street. It was about 2.5 miles from campus. It wasn't far from the variety store. He often bought beer and wine at the store.

He was walking home. He passed by an apartment where his former girlfriend lived. He wondered whether to knock on her door. They hadn't been an item for several months now. W wavered on whether to stop. He still had a thing for her. He really wanted to say hi. He decided he'd give it a try. He walked up to her door. He rang the doorbell. The door opened. It wasn't Donna Saylor. Donna was his old girlfriend. He hoped she would be home. It was her twin sister. It was Marybeth Saylor. She was not as pretty as Donna. She was more friendly.

"Hey W," Marybeth said. "What's goin' on?"

"Not much," W said. "Just thought I'd stop by."

"Donna's not here, sorry," Marybeth told Bush.

"That's OK," W said. "You're the one I always wanted anyway." He smiled.

"Right, right, W," Marybeth told him. "Come on in if you want. I'm just reading."

"I guess I'll head down to my apartment," he told her. "On the way to the package store. Matter of fact, you oughta stop by. I'm gonna pick up some beer."

"Really," Marybeth said. "Ya know what? I just might. When you gonna be there?"

"Gimme a half hour," W said.

"OK, great,' Marybeth said. "I'll see ya there in 'bout a half hour."

W dropped his books at his apartment. He drove down to the store to pick up some beer. He returned to his apartment with a case. He put the beer in the refrigerator. He took one out. He opened it. He sat down in an easy chair in his living room. He turned on the TV. He took a sip of the beer. He caught the end of a news report on a bloody firefight in Vietnam.

He shut off the TV. He took a big gulp of his Knickerbocker. He heard a knock on the door. He got up to answer it. "Hey, come on in, the water's fine," W said to Marybeth Saylor.

"Thanks W," she said. "I don't normally drink this early - in the day or in the week."

"Who said anything about your drinking?" W asked.

"Good one, W," she said.

"Now, sit down and lemme get you a beer, girl," he said. "Or maybe I should say, lemme get you a beer, sailor, you know, s, a, i, l, o, r?"

"Good .," Marybeth Saylor said. "Very funny. Yeah, I'll have one. But don't tell Donna."

W went in to the kitchen. He would get Marybeth a beer. "Why would I tell Donna?" he asked. "More to the point, what would I tell Donna. Hell, you're having a beer. Big fucking deal."

"Yeah, I guess so," Marybeth said. "Think she'll be jealous?"

"Of what - your having a beer?" W asked. He knew what Marybeth meant.

"Well, that too," she said. "But how 'bout us?"

"How about us?" W asked.

"Don't want Donna to know I'm fraternizing with you," her sister said.

"I really don't think she would care, Bush said. "And if she does, screw her. I don't really care if she cares. Here, drink up."

He tossed her a can of beer. "Whadda ya' think of this war?" W asked. He sat back down in the living room.

"The war?" Marybeth asked. "What prompts this? Oh, OK."

Bush explained to his friend. He said he was afraid he would lose his school deferment. He would be subject to the draft. The fear of combat was staring a lot of students Bush's age in the face. A lot of them were looking for ways to avoid it. If they had a school deferment, they were lucky. A lot of young men were too poor uneducated to go on to college. They had no real choice. For them it was either get a good education or get caught in Vietnam. Bush was lucky. Time was running out though. In just a few short weeks, he'd be facing reality. He hadn't made any plans for grad school. There was only one immediate, obvious option. It was the National Guard.

"Can't your father get you in?" Marybeth Saylor asked him. She took a sip on her beer.

"We're workin' on it," W said. He tossed his empty far across the room. It flew toward a wastebasket. "Lemme get another beer." He got up. He went in to the kitchen. He opened the refrigerator. He fetched another beer. It was his third in less than two hours.

W returned to the living room. The phone rang. Bush had a beer in his hand. He walked over to the phone. He picked up the receiver. "Your dime my time," he said.

"Junior," said a voice on the other end.

"Hey Poppy," W said. It was his father on the phone. Congressman George Bush was calling.

"We just heard back from the Pentagon," Congressman Bush said. "I think we're gonna be able to pull something off. I've got a contact for you at Ellington - the Air Force base. I think they're gonna make a spot for you. But you've got to call them. I can't."

"Big time," W said. He was excited. "Gimme the number Pops."

The elder Bush provided his eldest son with a phone number at the base. The Texas Air National Guard flew fighter jets out of that base. W's father explained to his son. He said recruits were trained first. They were often assigned to fly Corsair F-102s after their training.

"Hot shit, dad," W said. He quietly took a sip of his beer. "You think they'll take me?"

"Why the hell not?" his father the congressman replied. "Somebody's gotta! No, seriously, I think we've got a good shot at this."

W and his father ended their conversation. W hung up the phone. Marybeth Saylor had been listening to one side of the conversation. She sensed W had just received good news from his father.

W sat back down. He looked at her. He raised his can of beer. "Cheers," he said. "We're on a roll. Hey, isn't that what pilots say?"

"Tell me, what'd he say, what'd your father say?" she asked.

"He told me to call Ellington Air Force Base," W said. "Actually, call Houston. Sounds like I may not get my ass shot off after all."

"Then call them," Saylor said. "Might as well call 'em right now, right?"

"Good idea," W said. "Glad I thought of it."

Bush jumped up. He still had a beer in his hand. He dialed the number that his father had just given him. The phone rang twice. A woman answered. "Texas Air National Guard," she said. "May I help you?"

"You sure can," W said. "I am calling for Capt. Douglas Billiard."

"Uh, oh, Doug Bullard," the woman said.

"Bullard, Billiard, whatever," W said. "Thanks for the cue."

The woman didn't laugh at first. Then a second later she seemed to get the play on words. "OK, is he expecting your call?" she asked Bush.

"I sure hope so," W said. "No, yeah, I think he is, seriously. I'm Bush. George Bush."

"Oh!" she said. "Congressman!"

"No, no," W replied. "I'm actually his kid. I'm George W. Bush. He is George H.W. Bush. Same name, two different people."

"Oh, OK," the woman said. "I apologize for the error. Lemme put you through to Capt. Bullard, Mr. Bush."

"Hello, Capt. Bullard speaking," Bullard said.

"Hi captain, this is George Bush calling," W said.

"Oh, hi Mr. Bush," Bullard responded. "I was expecting your call. I understand you're looking for a billet this spring. I'm saving a spot for you."

"Oh, that's fantastic, sir," W said. He was holding his beer. "I can't thank you enough."

"Our pleasure, sir," Bullard said. "I'm going to forward you some paperwork. It'll all be self-explanatory. You'll just have to sign it. Drop it back in the mail to me. There'll be an envelope provided. Seal it when you're done. Drop it in the mail. Then we'll plan on seeing you at Ellington in late May. You'll see all this on the paperwork I'm sending you."

"Excellent, captain. You're the best," Bush replied. He gave Bullard his address at Yale.

"OK, sir, if you have any questions you don't hesitate to call on me," Bullard said. "Please send our best to Congressman Bush."

"Will do, captain, thanks again," W said. "Bye now."

W toasted Saylor. He raised his beer can. "This Air Force captain just basically told me I won't get my ass shot off in Vietnam," Bush told Saylor. "That's worth an extra toast. We'll have several toasts."

He had now drunk four beers. He got up out of the chair. He walked over to Saylor. He gave her a kiss on the left cheek.

"I'm honored," Saylor told Bush. She blushed. "Congratulations on the Air Guard. Wow, that's great."

"Thanks Saylor," W said.

"Wonder what my sister would say?" Saylor asked.

"About what?" W asked.

"Your kissing me, George," Saylor replied.

"Oh, kiss this," he said. "Who cares what your sister says? I told you. You were always the one I wanted anyway."

George W. Bush made it through finals. He made it to graduation. In mid-May 1968, the Vietnam War was raging. The son - and grandson - of privilege accepted a diploma. It showed he had earned a Bachelor of Arts degree in history. He had a diploma from a prestigious university. Commencement was held. Bush packed up his belonging. He headed up to Maine. He planned to spend a week in Maine. He would then fly to Texas. He would report for training at Ellington Air Force Base. There would be no summer vacation this year. Even the privileged lose out. George W. Bush was signing up for the Texas Air National Guard. Giving up a summer vacation in Kennebunkport was a big deal for him. Many youngsters his age were getting shot that same summer in Vietnam.

Everything is relative.

The Bushes were accustomed to pulling rank. George W. Bush's father used his political connections to make sure his eldest son never saw combat in Vietnam. He used his father's political influence to his own advantage. Former U.S. Sen. Prescott Bush had done the same for his son. George H.W. Bush was elected to the U.S. House in 1966. His got his son a seat on the House Ways and Means Committee. It was the most powerful committee in Washington. The panel was hard to get a seat on. Freshmen lawmakers usually had to fight for these positions.

George H.W. Bush was in his first term. His father again met with top GOP officials. He lobbied to get his son on the ticket with Richard Nixon. Prescott Bush and several other influential Republicans didn't have influence enough. Even former President Dwight Eisenhower's prestige wasn't enough. Nixon decided against choosing George H.W. Bush as his running mate. Nixon said Bush didn't have enough experience in public office.

George H.W. Bush had served nearly two terms in the Congress. He decided to make a second attempt at statewide office in Texas. He ran against U.S. Sen. Ralph Yarborough. It was 1970. Congressman Bush had made sure his son would never see combat. Now he would rely on that same child. W would work for him in his 1970 U.S. Senate campaign. It would require W to go AWOL from some of the meetings at the Texas Air National Guard. Meeting attendance was mandatory. It was a condition of continued service.

"Don't worry about it," Congressman Bush told his wife.

She expressed concern. "I'm worried," she said. She thought their eldest son might get in trouble. Barbara Bush didn't want him to spend too much time on the latest campaign. He would miss the mandatory meetings at the Texas Air National Guard.

"He's a Bush," his father argued. "There won't be any problems. I'll put a call in over there. I'll straighten out their asses."

"If you say so," Barbara Bush replied. "I just don't want Georgie to get in trouble. That's all we need. You're the one who wants that Senate seat. We can't get caught pulling strings for Georgie. He can't miss Guard meetings. That'll be the end of that."

It was hard to tell. Was she was concerned for her son? Was she worried about her husband? She'd expressed hope that her son wouldn't get in trouble. She didn't want him to miss Guard meetings to campaign for her husband. She said also her son could hurt her husband's campaign. She was a political wife. Barbara Bush couldn't win for trying.

It was worse. She had to put on a façade. She had to be a dutiful, doting, supportive wife of a congressman and candidate for the U.S. Senate. She was always moving. She had to follow her husband. His career was hers. It wasn't by her choice. She raised five children too. She was the hardest-working Bush.

George H.W. Bush admired his eldest son's political antennae. It was time again to put his name on a ballot. He turned to George W. Bush. W was now serving in the Texas Air National Guard. He took part in a cozy deal put together by his congressional father. The elder Bush's designs were on the White House. First he would have to pay his dues. It meant doing time. Lyndon Johnson once told him serving in the U.S. House was "chicken shit." He spoke of the Senate as "chicken salad." The point wasn't lost on Bush.

Bush had failed in his 1964 U.S. Senate bid against Yarborough. He had done his time in the House. He decided to run again for the upper chamber. He needed help. A second campaign against Yarborough would be hard.

Bush announced for the U.S. Senate on Jan. 13, 1970.

"George, I'm gonna need your help if you can break free," George H.W. Bush told his son.

Bush assumed he'd be running against Yarborough. Former Texas Congressman Lloyd Bentsen ruined that plan. Bentsen was an insurance executive in Houston. He challenged Yarborough. Bentsen won the Democratic primary. Now it was going to be Bentsen vs. Bush.

"Pop, I'm gonna see whether I can get out of some of these bullshit training sessions," George W. Bush told his father. They met in Houston in mid-July 1970.

"What do you think would happen if you missed a few sessions?" the senatorial-hopeful asked his eldest son. W had already received preferential treatment. He got into the Guard with dad's help. "Suppose anyone would notice?"

"Dunno, Pop," W replied. "Guess there's one way to find out, huh?"

"I suppose we could give it a try," his father replied. "I do need some help."

"Well, why don't I - " his son replied.

His father interrupted. "Look, who do you report to at these training drills?" his father asked. "Hell, I might as well call ahead. We can avoid problems. Bentsen's tough enough. We can't let this blow up."

The elder Bush was worried. He thought helping his son might backfire. It would be used against him. Bentsen was a tough opponent. The question was which he was more concerned about. Was it his Senate race? Would his son fail to meet his obligations to the Texas Air National Guard? Was he concerned his son might end up in Vietnam? No one will ever know. George H.W. may not know. The truth may elude him.

"Ware," W replied. "Lt. Donald Ware. I'm assuming he's the guy you'd need to talk to. He's basically in charge of keeping track who's coming to these training drills. Here, I'll jot down his number."

W grabbed a piece of scratch paper from the kitchen counter. He wrote down Ware's number. He handed it to his father.

"OK," George H.W. Bush said. "I'll give him a call. Someone in my office might do it."

Congressman Bush called his Capital Hill office. He asked for Bruce Choate. Choate was his chief of staff. "Bruce, it's George," Bush said.

"Hello, sir," Choate replied. "What can I do to help?"

"Bruce, can you call W's supervisor for me?" Congressman Bush asked his chief of staff. "I need Junior's help on this damn campaign. He's so tied up with his Guard drills. There isn't much time for strategizing against Bentsen. George is good at that kind of stuff. I could really use his help."

"Sure, sir," Choate replied. "Lemme give him a call. I'll do it right now."

"Oh, that would be great, Bruce," Bush said. He gave Choate Ware's name. He provided his phone number at Ellington. Ellington was the air base. "If there seems to be any hesitation on his part, well, hell, you know how to handle these things Bruce," Bush said. "Use your good judgment."

The two men hung up the phone. Senior Bush seemed pretty confident. He figured the Texas Air National Guard would spring his kid to do some campaign work. Senior Bush's hoped the Bentsen campaign wouldn't get wind of this. The elder Bush knew that Bentsen was a former congressman. Bentsen was a wealthy businessman. He had probably pulled several such stunts in his day. Politicians do it to protect constituents or clients. This was a high-stakes campaign for a coveted seat. This was a fight for the United States Senate. All bets were off. Gentlemanly politics were out the window.

Choate dropped everything. He closed the door to his office. He put in a call to the Texas Air National Guard.

The phone rang. Someone answered it at the Ellington Air Force Base outside of Houston. "Hello, this is Congressman George Bush's office calling for Lt. Donald Ware," Choate said.

"Good day sir," said a voice on the other end. "This is Sgt. Charles Hazard. I am Lt. Ware's executive officer. Would you like to talk to Lt. Ware?" "Yes, that would be great, sir," Choate said. "I would be glad to talk to you."

"I'd be glad to put Lt. Ware on," Hazard said. "He would be privileged to speak with you."

"Thank you sergeant," Choate replied. "My name is Bruce Choate. I am Congressman Bush's chief of staff. I am calling from Washington."

"OK, Mr. Choate, very fine, one moment please," Hazard said.

He put Choate momentarily hold. He passed the call through. He told his boss who was calling.

Ware picked up the phone. "Bruce Choate, how are ya'," Ware said. "Don Ware here. What can I do to help?"

Choate was taken aback by Ware's informality. He was put at ease. "Hi, lieutenant," Choate said. "Really appreciate your taking my call. The congressman asked me to inquire. He wants to know whether his son can spend some time on his father's senatorial campaign. He just wants to make sure he won't be punished if he misses a drill."

"I don't see a big problem," Ware said. "As long as we know a day or two in advance we're OK. That way we can fill his seat with somebody else."

Choate expressed his appreciation to Ware. He said he would pass on the information to Congressman Bush. Choate sensed that Ware wouldn't let George W. Bush miss drills just for the sake of missing drills. Ware was informal. But he took assignments seriously. He would be willing once in a while to bend a rule. He didn't want to make it a habit. Influential politicians seeking favors could be trouble.

Choate called his boss in Houston. He explained that the Guard would give the younger Bush an occasional pass on drills. He said such absences were to be rare. Congressman Bush seemed surprised. He didn't want qualifications placed on his request. He also knew he was asking for a special favor. An average member of the Texas Air National Guard wouldn't receive such treatment.

"Bruce, thanks much," Congressman Bush told Choate. "Sounds like they're a bit sensitive out there to this. Hell, maybe I ought to call 'em myself." "You are welcome to do that sir," Choate said. "I would leave it as it is. If the time comes when you need your son more often than his training schedule would permit, then press the issue."

As a congressional chief of staff, Choate knew boundaries. He was deferential when he needed to be. He was frank when he needed to be. In this case, he felt he needed to let his boss know just where things stood. Otherwise the younger Bush's help on the campaign could be in trouble. His standing in the Air National Guard could be in jeopardy.

George W. Bush tried to help get his father elected to the U.S. Senate. It didn't work. Bentsen defeated George H.W. Bush. Bentsen beat the Republican congressman from Texas' Seventh District with 53 percent of the vote. The elder Bush had chosen to give up his U.S. House seat. Now he was out of a job. He blamed the loss partly on Democrats in the rural parts of his adopted home state. They came out in droves for Bentsen. They believed the election would help liberalize the state's laws governing the sales of alcoholic beverages. It was ironic. The elder Bush blamed his loss on drinkers. He had alcoholism in his family. His son was now a pilot in the Texas Air National Guard.

Young George W. Bush took his father's electoral defeat to heart. It was his father's second failed attempt at statewide office in six years

The son felt he had let down the father. His father had gone out of his way to make sure Junior was sprung from some of his air drills. W helped the campaign. The elder Bush had placed his political life in jeopardy.

George W. Bush drank heavily on election night that November, 1970. It was his usual behavior. It didn't matter whether his father won or lost. W would be drinking. He'd celebrate a victory with alcohol. He'd drown his defeats in whiskey. There was always an excuse for a drink.

George W. Bush left the Houston hotel. His family was there for the election results. He drove home. He had been drinking Jim Beam. The night wore on. The votes for Bentsen mounted. The Jim Beam flowed freely.

He headed out of the hotel parking lot. He nearly hit a doorman. The doorman was standing sentry at the gated entrance to the lot. W nearly struck a light pole that marked the boundary of the entrance.

He finally got out of the lot. W picked up from the car seat a goblet with ice and Jim Beam. It was precariously balanced. He negotiated his way out of the hotel parking lot.

"Here's to shit," he said to himself. He raised the glass.

He drove home. The car radio was blaring. This was the Yale-educated grandson of a former U.S. senator. This was a fighter-plane pilot son of a U.S. congressman. He had heavy on his mind his father's uncertain future. He wasn't worried about his own. He was worried about his father's. He felt an obligation to his father. It didn't matter that their relationship was strained. He felt a call to duty. His father had protected him. Papa Bush kept him from Vietnam combat. Now it up to the son to return the favor. But he was worried now. What would his father do for work? His father had given up a congressional seat. He had thought he could beat Ralph Yarborough for the U.S. Senate. But Bentsen came out of the woodwork. All bets were off. Now, George H.W. Bush was two months away from being unemployed. His son felt responsible for it.

Chapter VIII
Touch Your Nose

George W. Bush had gotten out of his Texas Air National Guard obligation. He left six months early to attend Harvard Business School. It was another instance of his father's political connections serving him well.

He made good money after entering the oil business in Texas. It was in the mid 1970s. But W wasn't happy. He still felt he was making it in his father's shadow. His success wasn't his own. He also attributed any of his failures to his father. A complicated dynamic represented their relationship. His father had lost in 1970 loss to Lloyd Bentsen. The U.S. Senate seat from Texas had eluded him. W was anxious. He was worried about himself. He was wondering what his father would do. It's almost as if he wanted to find his father a satisfying job. Then he could turn to his own search for personal peace and prosperity. The senior Bush hopped from one job to the next. They were mostly political payback jobs. George H.W. Bush had lost to Bentsen. He was given a booby prize by President Nixon. It was the UN ambassadorship. Two years passed. It was 1973. He became chairman of the Republican National Committee.

That's where he met Jennifer Fitzgerald. Fitzgerald was his secretary. W at the time was in a tailspin. Professionally and personally his life was a confusion. He didn't find his work fulfilling. He hadn't met a woman. He wanted to settle down. He wanted to start a family. He started hearing rumors about his father. He was having an affair. W wasn't sure what to make of it.

Fitzgerald was a young divorcee. The senior Bush had brought her to China. She helped him run the U.S. Liaison Office in Beijing. The elder Bush's wife, Barbara, was often with him in China. There were periods when she was gone. Sometimes she flew back to the U.S. She left her husband alone.

George W. Bush didn't want to believe his father was having an affair. But he couldn't ignore the gossip. It involved his father and Jennifer Fitzgerald. W believed his mother had never gotten over the loss from leukemia of her daughter

Robin. The only thing that could be more devastating to her would be believing her husband wasn't being faithful to her. W never brought up the subject with his mother. He confronted his father with the question one time.

It was late in the summer 1976. George H.W. Bush had been in his latest patronage job. He was director of the Central Intelligence Agency. He'd held the job six months. He was telling everyone how much he liked the job. Of course, there was only one job he really wanted. He wanted to be president of the United States.

It was July 4th, 1976. The extended Bush family was celebrating the holidays. They often did at the family compound. Along the ocean in Kennebunkport, Maine was a nice place to be. It was idyllic. Children scampered about. They played in the summer sun. adults swam in the ocean and in the pool. The men went boating and fishing.

George W. Bush was also spending time in Maine away from Texas. He had been brooding. The rumors about his father's alleged extramarital affair with a young secretary were tearing at him. He wondered to what extent his mother was paying attention to the issue. He hoped she had no idea about the rumors.

"I'm headed downtown," W told his mother. He left the oceanfront home that Saturday afternoon.

"Don't wanna go out fishing with Pop?" Barbara Bush asked her eldest son. He breezed through the kitchen.

"No," W answered curtly. He said not another word. He headed out the door. He jumped in to the rental car. He had picked it up at the airport in Portland. He drove downtown. He found a space behind Allison's. It was his favorite bar. He parked the car. He walked around the front of the restaurant. He went inside. W ran into Dean Annison. Annison's family lived just down the road. They lived on Ocean Avenue. They weren't far from the Bush's.

Annison was sitting at one of the small tables. He was near the front of the restaurant. His window seat overlooked Dock Square.

"Hey W," Annison said. "Sit down."

"Deano-boy," W replied. "How's it hangin'?"

"Jesus, George Bush, I haven't seen you for awhile," Annison said. He stood up. He gave W a solid handshake.

"Sit down, boy," W said. "We're got some serious drinking to do."

"I can see you haven't changed," Annison said. He took a bite of his bacon cheeseburger.

"Change this," W said. "Where's the broad who's working this table?"

"She's over there," Annison said. "She'll be back."

"Time's a wastin'," W said. "I'm thirsty." He yelled to the waitress, "Hey can we get some action over here?" The waitress held up her finger indicating she'd be right over. In a few seconds, she came over to the table.

"Hi, can I get something for you?" she asked Bush.

"Yeah, you can get something for me," he said. He smiled. "I'll have a pitcher of whatever you've got on draft."

"OK," she said. "Anything else?"

"What's your name?" W asked.

"Melanie," she replied.

"Melanie who?" W asked.

"Melanie Mayer," she said.

"OK, so what'd they call you, M-squared?" he asked.

"George, give the girl a break," Annison pleaded.

"OK," W said.

The waitress left the table. She went to get Bush's beer. He yelled to her. "Hey M-squared, how 'bout a shot of Jim Beam too?"

"OK," she said. "Be right there."

The waitress returned to W's table. She balanced a tray on her left hand. She had a pitcher of beer, two beer mugs and a shot of Jim Beam. "Here you go," she said. She set the beer, mugs and shot glass on the small table.

"Thanks M-squared," W. said, He smiled "Will you join us?"

"Sorry," Mayer said. "The boss would kill me."

"And your point is?" W asked.

"Melanie, don't mind him," Annison said. He apologized for W's boorish behavior. "He's harmless."

Bush picked up the shot glass. He raised it to Annison. "Happy Fourth, Deano" he said. He tossed the shot of Jim Beam into his mouth. He picked up the pitcher. He filled his mug with cold draft beer. He also poured a glass of beer for Annison. He picked up his mug. He raised it to his friend. He began slugging it down.

"Jesus, slow down boy," Annison said.

"No time to," W said. "Man that tastes good. Hey Deano, lemme ask you somethin'.."

"Shoot," Annison responded.

"Your father ever screw around on your mom?" Bush asked.

"What?" Annison asked. He was dumbfounded at W's question.

"You heard me," W said. "Just tell me."

"Christ, I dunno George," Annison said. "Why would you ask me that?"

"Because I'm worried about Mummsy," W said. He took a big swig of beer. He emptied his mug.

"Why?" Annison asked. W began filling up his mug again from the pitcher. "What's up?"

"Just a second, Deano," Bush said. "Hey, can we get another pitcher?" he yelled to the waitress. She was halfway across the room. She nodded in acknowledgment.

"Have you heard some of this shit about my father?" W asked Annison.

"What shit?" Annison asked.

"Christ, Deano, it's been in some of the rag. There are stories about Dad having an affair. It's a secretary."

"I don't know what you're talking about W," Annison said.

"Well," W said. "Supposedly Dad's been spending a lot of time with some chick. She worked for him at the RNC. She followed him to China. They supposedly go off on junkets together. Supposedly no one's ever caught them in bed. Where there's smoke there's fire."

The waitress brought over another pitcher of beer. She also brought a second shot of Jim Beam for W.

"Thanks chickie," W said. He filled up his mug. He poured the shot of Jim Beam down his throat. He washed it down with half a mug of beer.

George W. Bush was filling himself with liquid courage. He anticipated the moment. He would confront his father. He would ask the big question. Was his father screwing Jennifer Fitzgerald?

It was now mid-afternoon. W and Annison had spent nearly two hours at their window seat in Allison's. They'd downed three pitchers of beer. Bush had also had two shots of Jim Beam.

"Shit, I gotta get goin'," Annison said.

"What, you got a hot date?" W asked.

"I wish," Annison said. "No, gotta help mother with some stuff. You gonna be around all weekend?"

"Yeah, unless I get thrown out," W said. "I'll catch ya' later. Wish me luck."

"Look, George, do what you gotta do," Annison said. "Why don't you gimme a call later."

The two split up/ W walked around the back of Allison's. He got to his car. He went to open the driver's door. He missed the door handle. He lost his balance. He nearly fell in the parking lot. He was able to regain his footing. He managed to drive back to the family compound. He parked out front. He got out of the car. His father was walking from the dock. He was headed to the boat shed. He had his fishing tackle in his hand.

W approached his father. He didn't say anything.

"Where you been?" George H.W. Bush asked his son. "Shudda come fishin' with us. Some nice blues out there."

"I was down at Allison's," W replied. "I need to talk to you." He was curt. He addressed his father. His father was then the CIA director.

Rarely did W make such a serious overture to his father. Usually it was his father saying to his son he had to talk.

He got near his father. He said, "I'm really worried about something Pops."

"What's wrong," the elder Bush asked.

"Dad, I'm sick over all this talk about some woman," W said.

"Huh?" his father asked.

"This woman. What's her name? Jennifer something," W said.

His father looked at him sternly. "You've been drinking," George H.W. Bush said to his son. He avoided the Jennifer question.

"Doesn't matter what I've been doing," W said. "I wanna know."

"You wanna know what, Junior?" his father asked. He called him Junior to piss off his eldest son. He was no junior. His middle initial wasn't his father's.

"I wanna know who Jennifer is?" W persisted.

"You show some respect," his father said. "Get off it."

"Get off what?" W asked. He pushed up to his father's face.

W took a swing at his father. He grazed his father's right cheek. He fell on the rocks. "You asshole," W shouted at his father.

George H.W. Bush knew this was not the place to debate. His son was drunk. He wouldn't discuss whether he was having an affair. He wasn't going to dignify the allegation. He wouldn't answer his son's grilling. The elder Bush wanted this discussion to end. Quickly. Before anyone else got involved. He continued on to the boat shed. He left his son on the ground. He ignored his son's obscenity-laced tirade against the nation's CIA director.

George H.W. Bush walked away. A Secret-Service agent was removing seat cushions from the boat. He ran over. His name was Ray Button.

"Can we help, sir?" Button asked the elder Bush.

"Nah, no big deal," the elder Bush said. "Junior's been drinking. Been there, done that. Let him sleep it off."

W regained his footing. He was following his father to the boat shed.

"So is it true or isn't it?" W asked. His voice was rising.

"George, get off my ass," his father told his son. "You've got a problem. It's not me, boy. It's Jim Beam."

"Screw you," W said. "I'm going in to see Mummsy."

W walked in to the house. His mother was in the kitchen. She was arranging roses. She had a vase for her centerpiece.

"Where you been honey?" she asked her son. "You must be hungry."

"I ain't hungry Mummsy," W told his mother. He walked past her. He headed to his bedroom.

She smelled his breath. She knew he had been drinking. She thought this was no time to discuss his drinking problem. It was growing increasingly chronic by the year. Her son was now 29. In two days - July 6 - he would mark his 30th birthday. The Bush family typically celebrated W's birthday in Kennebunkport. That was the time of year the clan would be in Maine.

W got to his room. He slammed the door shut. He threw off his loafers. He lay down. He laid on his back. The sound of the ocean lapped at the back shore of the house. He stared at the ceiling. His head was spinning. The booze made him dizzy. He felt sick. He was nauseous. He had just had a physical confrontation with his father. His father may be two-timing his mother.

That was bad enough. His father wouldn't deny the accusation. His son decided it was true.

"Honey, what kind of a cake would you like this year?" Barbara Bush yelled from the kitchen. She wanted to make W a birthday cake.

"I don't want a cake," W yelled back.

"Of course you'll have a cake," she said. "It's your birthday. 30 years old. Can you believe it?"

W loved his mother. He was sick over his father. He couldn't bear to ask his mother about some woman. A woman named Jennifer. "How about chocolate, Mummsy?" W asked his mother.

"One chocolate birthday cake comin' up," Barbara Bush yelled.

George W. Bush was having a birthday cake. He didn't want one. He knew how much it would mean for his mother to bake him a birthday cake. She had done it each year since he was born. She did the same with the other kids.

Barbara Bush began getting out the ingredients for the cake. From a canister on the countertop she removed four cups of flour. She put them in a mixing bowl. She took out sugar and powdered cocoa from the cupboard. She took milk, butter and eggs from the refrigerator. She was arranging the items on the counter. Her husband came through the door.

"Junior is some condition," George H.W. Bush said to his wife. "Just let him be until he sobers up."

"What is going on with him George?" Barbara Bush asked her husband. "His drinking is out of control."

"No idea," the senior Bush said. "He's gonna have to work through it. I gotta jump in the shower."

He just kept on walking. He went down a hall. He got to his and Barbara's bedroom. He began getting ready to take a shower. He sat down on the side of the bed. He began taking off his boating shoe. He stopped as he reached down to remove his right shoe. "What am I gonna do?" he asked himself.

What wasn't clear. Was he talking about his alcoholic son or Jennifer?

The elder Bush needed to provide an answer for his eldest son. W might continue to press the issue. He might get drunk again. All bets were off.

Barbara might find out.

It was 6 that night. Barbara Bush had prepared a birthday cake for a celebration. She made a lobster supper for the whole family. The family included relatives of the extended Bush clan. It also included two Secret-Service agents. By law they protected the director of the CIA. George H.W. Bush had around-the –clock security.

"Soup's on," Barbara yelled. She also opened the front door. She yelled to all who were outside playing.

W came out of his room. He had been sleeping off his latest drunk.

"What's the matter, Georgie been partying too hard?" his sister Doro asked him. She teased her big brother.

W.'s father came into the dining room. His eldest son had just taken a seat. George H.W. Bush wouldn't look his eldest son in the eye.

W said nothing. He was drunk before. His father's alleged affair was a big deal. Now he was sober. He wasn't ready to press the issue.

The big group took seats at the table. Barbara Bush was serving the side dishes. Her husband was passing out the lobsters. It was such an idyllic family scene. The family was on the shore of the Atlantic in Kennebunkport, Maine. It would have been Norman Rockwell on the July Fourth holiday. But the Bushes had money.

The son of the director of the CIA was an alcoholic. He was pressing the director of the CIA into admitting whether he was committing adultery.

The July Fourth holiday ended. The Bush clan went their separate ways. W went back to Texas He would play the oil industry. George and Barbara Bush went back to Washington, DC. The elder Bush was holding court at the CIA. He was collecting political chits. He fantasized an ascendancy someday soon to the Oval Office.

W arrived in Texas. He met with one of his business partners. He and John Niely would discuss an investment they had made. A small oil company showed a lot of promise. Its focus was research-and-development. They met at their offices for an hour. W suggested they go downtown for a drink. It was nearly 5 p.m. He was thirsty. They ended up at Mulligan's. It was an Irish pub on Midland's south side. The bar was a popular hangout for a lot of influential Midland businessmen. George W. Bush had made some good business and political contacts beginning in the early 1970s. He ordered himself a shot of Jim Beam. He also asked for two drafts. Niely asked for a draft.

"Here's to ya'," W said. He toasted his friend. Niely joined the toast.

Five minutes passed. W had tossed down both shots of Jim Beam and a large mug of draft beer. He was already calling the waitress over to re-order. He also ordered another draft for Niely.

"Hey Johnny, I'm gonna head up to Maine for Labor Day if you feel like joining me," W told his drinking and business pal. "We usually close up the cottage. We put the boats up about then. Been awhile since you were up there."

"Might just join you, "Niely replied. "Any chicks up there?"

"Oh sure, all over Kennebunkport," W said. "Lots of babes. We're sure to meet some at Allison's. It's a drinking joint downtown."

They made tentative plans for the Labor Day holiday. They had had a few beers and shots. W left Mulligan's. Niely left too. They headed to their respective homes. W decided to call his sister.

"Doro, what's with all this stuff I'm hearing about Pops," W said. His sister picked up the phone in Washington.

"What do you mean?" she asked her older brother.

"I've been reading and hearing about some woman that dad is allegedly having an affair with," W said. "Jennifer somebody."

"Oh Georgie, that's Jennifer Fitzgerald," W's sister replied. "She's worked for dad a long time. You know her."

"Oh, that Jennifer," W said. So what's the deal?"

"I'm assuming it's just tabloid trash," Doro said. She wasn't necessarily dismissing the possibility out of hand. She said she assumed it wasn't true.

"You gonna be up Labor Day?" W asked.

"Yeah, I guess so," she said. "I assume you're coming up?"

"10-4," W said. "I'll talk to you more then."

It was the first week in September. W had made plans. He would head up to Maine. He'd be there Labor Day weekend. He and his business partner, John Niely, flew to Portland, Maine. They rented a car. They drove down the coast. They arrived in Kennebunkport.

They arrived there on Sept. 3. Most of the Bush family was there. They arrived Sept. 2. W decided to head down to Allison's. He took Niely with him. They would go to W's favorite bar.

They took a table near the back of the restaurant. It gave them an expansive view. They could see anyone who would walk in.

"Hey W!" someone shouted from behind the bar. "What can I getchya?"

"A fifth of Jim Beam," W yelled back. "And a pitcher of draft to wash it down."

"On its way," came the reply. Bush's friend was tending bar. Bush had known Harry Millikin since they were kids. Millikin sent over an eight-ounce goblet of Jim Beam. He also ordered a pitcher of beer.

Niely looked down. He shook his head. He laughed. He knew George W. Bush. His alcohol-consumption quotient was legendary. He saw the bartender send over a goblet filled to the brim with bourbon.

"Happy Favor Day," W said. He raised the glass of bourbon. He addressed Niely. He used one of his favorite colloquialisms. He referred to Labor Day. He had once decided that since Labor Day meant a no-work holiday, it was a favor. W took a gulp of Jim Beam. He put down the glass. He hefted his beer mug. He washed down the hard stuff with the beer. He shook his head when the process was done.

Niely took a sip of beer. He noticed a woman at a nearby table. She looked in Bush's direction. She smiled. "Hey George, who's that?" Niely asked. He nodded in the woman's direction. "She seems to know you."

"Beats me," W said, laughing. "Beat this baby."

Time wore on. Bush's consumption was increasing. The alcohol was getting ahead of him. He had downed nearly all of the Jim Beam. He also drank three mugs of beer. Niely had two beers. He said he was ready to head back to the Bush compound.

"You go ahead," W said. "I'll catch up with you later." Niely took Bush up on his offer. They had only brought one car. Niely called Twin City Taxi. They sent a cab over to Allison's. Niely left Bush. He went outside to wait for the cab. An hour passed. It was just before midnight. W polished off the Jim Beam. He took one last swallow of the remaining beer. It was the bottom of the pitcher. He reached in to his pocket. He pulled out a wad of cash. He left it on the table. He got up to leave Allison's. He yelled to his friend behind the bar.

"Harry, keep it in your sneaker," W shouted. "There's some money on the table. Take some of it for yourself. Maybe you'll get laid later."

W walked out of Allison's. He went around the back. He found his car. He reached for his keys. He finally found the key to the car. He opened the driver's door. He fell in to the sea. He inserted the key. He started the car. He headed out of the parking lot. He ran over the curb in process. He drove up Ocean Avenue.

The downtown was fairly desolate. Many summer tourists left in late August. Bush's was among the few cars on the road. He went down Ocean Avenue. He headed toward his family's oceanside compound. He noticed a car in his rear-view mirror.

"Stay cool," he told himself. He was afraid. He thought it might be a cop. He turned left. He followed a curve in the road. W overcompensated. He tried to straighten out the wheel. He figured he would stop to get his bearings. He pulled over briefly. He drove on the shoulder of the road. He pulled out again. He resumed his direction of travel.

Twenty seconds passed. W saw blue lights. They were behind him. He looked in his rear-view mirror. He realized a police car was behind him. He pulled over. An officer got out of the cruiser. He came up to W's door. The window was already down.

"Do you know why I stopped you sir?" the officer asked Bush. The officer was Calvin Bridges. He knew who Bush was.

"Uh, not sure," W replied.

"I noticed some erratic operation," Bridges said. "Could I see your license and registration?"

"Sure," W said. He pulled out his license from his back pocket. He handed the officer the registration. W found the registration in the glove box.

"OK," the officer said. "I'd like you to get out of the vehicle. I need to give you a sobriety test."

Bush got out of the car. Bridges told him to extend his arms perpendicular to his torso. He told him to close his eyes.

"With your eyes closed, please touch the tip of your nose with your right forefinger," Officer Bridges requested. Bush missed his nose. He touched his lower lip with his forefinger.

Bridges asked Bush to walk forward. He told him to put one foot directly in front of the other. Bush complied. He almost fell over.

"I have to place you under arrest for suspicion of operating a motor vehicle while under the influence," Bridges told Bush.

"OK," Bush said.

Bridges called a tow truck. The truck came from Arundel Auto. It would pick up W's car. Bridges instructed the tow-truck driver to deliver the car to the Bush house. The house was a mile away on Ocean Avenue. Bridges placed Bush in handcuffs. He put him in the rear seat of his cruiser. Bridges got behind the wheel. He headed to the Kennebunkport Police Department. The station was on Crow Hill. It was a few miles past Bush's house.

Bridges pulled in to the police department parking lot. He stopped the car. He got out. He opened the left-rear passenger door. Bush was in handcuffs. He got out. Bush was usually the life of the party. Now he was silent. He said absolutely nothing. Bridges escorted him to the police station. They went in the side door. Bridges escorted Bush into an interrogation room. A breath test was administered.

The test showed Bush with a 0.10 percent blood-alcohol level. It was the legal threshold to prove a case of drunk driving.

"Sir, I have to charge you with OUI," Bridges told Bush. "I need you to sign this ticket. You acknowledge the charge. You can contest the charge by showing up Monday in Biddeford District Court. You can waive the contest and plead guilty."

W signed the warrant. Bridges released him on his own recognizance.

Bush shook Bridges' hand. He thanked him for his professionalism.

"I know you're just doing your job," W said. He stated the obvious. Bush walked out the door. He started walking to his parents' house. It was shortly after 1:45 a.m. W walked up the driveway. It led to the Bush compound. A Secret Service agent was on duty on the grounds. He was there because Bush's father was CIA director. The agent saw W approaching. He shined a bright flashlight in his eyes.

"Hey man, cool, it's me, W," Bush said. He was blinded by the light.

"OK, sir," the agent said. "Just makin' sure."

"They bring my car?" W asked.

"A wrecker dropped off a car here. It was a little while ago. He said it was yours, sir," the agent replied.

W walked in the front door. He went toward his bedroom.

He stopped by the liquor cabinet on the way. He grabbed a bottle. It was Jim Beam. He selected a small glass. He poured himself a couple shots. He corked the bottle. He went in to his room.

George H. W. Bush awoke on Sept. 5, 1976. He was at the family's Kennebunkport compound. He began preparing to fly back to Washington. He would have an intelligence briefing with President Nixon.; It was set for 1 p.m. He was preparing to make coffee for the members of the Bush family. He saw an envelope on his desk. It was marked "confidential." He opened the envelope. He found a report from the Secret Service. The agency generally avoided getting involved in the personal lives of those they protected.

"Mr. Director," the note said, "please see attached." It was the copy of George W. Bush's arrest report. It was supplied as a professional courtesy. The Kennebunkport Police Department furnished it. The senior Bush sat down. He had a coffee in his hand. He read the report. He was in shock.

His wife was still asleep. So was W. Bush didn't know what to do. He summoned his guard. The guard was in front of the house. His name was Ed Thompson.

"What do we know about this?" Bush demanded.

"Sir, all I know is what you see there," said Thompson. "It was passed on to me during the shift change this morning."

"Lord Jesus," the senior Bush said. "Arrested? How the hell? Do we know this cop? What's his name? Bridges. Calvin Bridges?"

"Sir, I'm not familiar," Thompson replied.

"Well who can we get on the phone over there?" Bush asked. "This is going to explode in my face. Get them on the phone now, please."

Thompson followed orders these came from the director of the CIA. Thompson didn't answer to the CIA. But he put a call in to the Kennebunkport Police Department. He identified himself. He asked to speak to the chief of police. The dispatcher put the chief on the phone. The chief was John Prescott.

"Good morning," Prescott said.

"Good morning chief," Thompson said. "Director Bush has asked me to get some details. His son was arrested."

"Oh, yes, I was just going over the run sheets," Prescott said. "I did see that Junior had been arrested. Let's see, it shows a court date for next week. He can plead or contest it."

"I guess Director Bush is wondering if, uh, well he just asked me to call you," Thompson said. He was fumbling for words. He didn't really understand what it was he was supposed to be doing. He was just told to call the police department.

"OK," the chief replied. "The arresting officer will be in around 4 if you need to talk to him."

"Thanks, Chief, I think we're all set," Thompson replied. He hung up.

Thompson went to brief the CIA director. He told the elder Bush he had called the police department.

"What did they say?" the director asked.

"The chief just basically summarized the arrest sheet for me," Thompson told Bush.

Bush nodded. He knew he couldn't directly ask the police to quash the arrest. He hoped the phone call from the Secret Service might help. He doubted it. The local police had a reputation of playing no favorites. The director of the Central Intelligence Agency wouldn't hold influence. If favoritism were their business, they'd never have arrested young George in the first place.

George H.W. Bush was about to leave the house. His driver was with him. He grabbed his briefcase. He ran into W in the hallway. It was between the living room and the bathroom. Father looked at son. Son looked at father.

The silence was deafening.

Neither of them said a word.

George H.W. Bush froze. He had no idea what he would say. His son was 30 years old. He wasn't a boy. The days of trying to discipline George W. Bush were gone. George W. Bush still lived in his father's shadow. He considered himself incorrigible. Drinking was his way of rebelling. He wouldn't listen to a lecture now. He might lecture his father instead. His father knew it. He could lecture W for his latest escapade. He knew his kid would start with the Jennifer thing.

It was a no-win for W's father. He just stared at his son.

His son stared back.

No words were spoken.

W's father walked out the door. He headed for the nation's capital.

W came out of the bathroom. His head hurt. He went to his bedroom. He sat down on the bed. He ran over in his mind the events of the night before. He didn't think it was a big deal. It was more a pain in the ass than anything else. He didn't want to have to trek into Biddeford. He would have to make an appearance in Maine District Court. It was a silly driving charge. He decided to call David Hirsch. Hirsch was an attorney friend of his father. He practiced law in Portland.

"Mr. Hirsch's office, can I help you?" asked a voice on the other end of the phone.

"It's George Bush," W said. "Lookin' to talk to Dave."

"Oh, hi Mr. Bush," said the woman who answered the phone. "Well, I'm not the Mr. Bush," W said. "It's W, George W. Bush."

"Oh, sure, Mr. Bush, let me get Mr. Hirsch for you," the woman said.

W didn't know whether the secretary understood what he was trying to tell her. He didn't care. He just wanted Hirsch.

"George?" Hirsch said. He picked up the phone.

"Dave, it's W," Bush replied. "I'm in some shit."

"What's up kid?" Hirsch asked.

"Cops got me last night," W said. "DWI."

"OK," Hirsch replied. "Where?"

"Down here," W said. "Oh, sorry, I'm in the 'Port. It happened on Ocean Avenue around the corner from the house."

"We can try to plead it down," Hirsch said. "Or we'll just make an appearance and be done with it."

"I just wanna pay the fine and be done with it," W said.

"Lemme make some calls," Hirsch said. "I'll let you know. Just drop the ticket in the mail to me. Those fines aren't usually that much. I'm guessing $150."

"Consider it done," W said. "I'll put it in the mail."

George W. Bush ended up pleading guilty to the charge of drunken driving. He paid a $150 fine. His right to drive in Maine was revoked until 1978. W headed back to Texas. He never looked back.

Chapter IX
Tee or Me

George W. Bush was sitting at a bar in Midland, Texas. An old boyhood friend came through the door.

"Hey asshole, sit down," W shouted. "I'll buy you a drink." He was shouting to Clifford Rivers. Rivers owned a Midland car dealership.

"W!" Rivers said. He walked over to the bar. "Don't mind if you do," he added.

"What'll ya' have bud?" Bush asked his friend. "Bud?"

"I'll have the same as you," Rivers said. "Jim Beam?"

"He's my good buddy, Jimmy Beam," W replied. "Barkeep, can we get another coupla' shots over here?"

The bartender poured the Jim Beam. W had already had several. He told Rivers friends were trying to fix him up "with some babe."

"Oh?" Rivers asked. "Who is it?"

"Laura somebody," W said. "Who knows? Might be worth a shot. Hey, speaking of shots, I'll match you two for one."

"Yuck, yuck, Junior," Rivers said. "Cheers." He raised his glass to Bush.

"Cheers to you Cliffy-boy," W. said. He raised his glass.

"So tell me," Rivers said. "Who's this they're trying to fix you up with?"

"Oh, her," W said. "Laura, I think her name is. Some teacher. I guess she's a librarian."

"Could be interesting," Rivers said. "You and a librarian. You know what they say old boy. Opposites attract."

"Long as she has a nice rack," W said. "I think she does. I do believe I met her a while back. She thought I was too political."

Rivers was married. He had children. He shook his head. "You never change," he told Bush.

W was taking a shower. He was getting ready for his big date. It was the fall of 1977. Bush's friends were fixing him up. His date would be a woman named Laura Welch. They were set to get together at a backyard barbecue. A month before Bush announced he was running for the U.S. House. He would represent Texas' Nineteenth Congressional District.

His plans to meet someone could round him out as a candidate. W had a shrewd political mind. His father later came to understand that. W knew that campaigning as a couple would help him. It would endear him to voters. They could then envision him as a family guy.

So what if he was a drunk.

"Oh, it's nice to see you," W said. He shook Laura Welch's hand. She shook his. They met at the barbecue.

"It's very nice to see you," Welch said.

"How 'bout a drink darlin'?" W said. He chuckled. He had a beer in his hand. He'd had one before that.

"Uh, sure, I'd be glad to have a beer," Welch said.

"Stick with me, baby," W said. "Come on over here." He brought her over to a cooler filled with beer. He fished one out for her. He opened the beer. He handed it to his date.

"So what's this I hear about you?" she asked.

"Dunno," he said. He laughed. "Depends on what you heard," he said.

"Are you running for Congress?" she asked.

"I'm runnin' for my life," W laughed. He took a big swig on his beer. "Uh, no, yeah, I am. Full speed ahead."

"Oh my," Welch said. "That is something."

"You can say that again," W said. "We'll see what happens. I think it's exciting."

"Why, I do too," Welch said. "I think it's very exciting."

W and Laura Welch hit it off splendidly. He was the outgoing socialite. She was the shy, demure librarian.

Their pasts were more alike in one tragic respect than they were different. George W. Bush as a child expressed that he was supposed to keep his mother happy. He said that after her young daughter, Robin, died of leukemia.

Laura Welch was an only child. Her mother wanted more children. She tried to have more children. But she suffered miscarriages.

George W. Bush was the namesake of the father. He was expected to carry on the elder's legacy.

Laura Welch was the only child. She felt obligated to succeed. She would be her mother's only pride.

It was the day after the barbecue. W called Laura Welch. She was at her Midland home. He was living in Midland too. It was her hometown. It was his adopted hometown.

"Hi," W said. She answered the phone. "It's Congressman George W. Bush."

"Hey, congressman," she replied. "Are we going campaigning today?"

Bush had only weeks before announced his candidacy. He was only a candidate at the time he first went out with Laura Welch.

"Got an idea," W said. "How 'bout some miniature golf?"

"Sounds like a good idea George," Welch said.

"OK, how about I stop by and pick you up?" he asked.

"Sounds like a line to me," Welch laughed.

"Well, if it works then I'm all for it," W said.

"Me, too," Welch replied. "Sure, what time?"

"How 'bout 2 o'clock?" W asked.

"Sure, I'll be here," Welch said.

Miniature golf sounded so un-Bush. If it involved having a few beers it would be more like his game. W got ready for his first real date with Laura Welch. He wondered whether to bring a six-pack. Normally he'd just buy the beer. George W. Bush was thinking about whether he should buy beer. It reflected on his not wanting to screw up what could be a perfect union.

He deliberated. Her decided he'd buy some beer. He would stop on the way.

Bush pulled in to Laura Welch's driveway. He shut off the car. He got out. He headed up sidewalk. He arrived at her front door. He rang the doorbell. He was nervous.

"Oh hi," Welch said. She opened the front door. "Come right in congressman," she said.

"Why thank you very much, ma'am," W replied. He walked in. "How'd you like to make some speeches?" he asked.

"Speeches?" she asked. "What kind of speeches?"

"Elect-George-Bush-to-congress speeches," W replied.

"Oh my god no," Welch said. "You're not serious."

"No I'm George W. Bush." He replied. "I'm running for Congress. I'm from the Nineteenth District. I'm from the great state of Texas."

"No, really, I don't need to make speeches do I?" she asked.

"Hell, no, 'course not," W said. "Just stand there and look pretty. You do that well."

Laura Welch blushed. "You're nice," she said. "Lemme just grab my bag and we'll be off." Welch retrieved a small purse from the bathroom. She paused. She made a check in the mirror. It was over her bathroom sink. She reached into her purse. She pulled out a tube of lipstick. She touched-up her lips.

"OK," she said. She returned to the living room. "We're ready to go."

W and Welch left the house. They headed down the sidewalk. They got to the car. W walked with Welch to the passenger side of the car. He opened the door for her.

"I'm quite impressed," she said. She smiled. "Chivalry lives. Thank you very much."

"Don't mention it," W said. He closed the door. He walked around the front of the car. He got in the driver's seat.

"If you're thirsty we've got some cold ones in the back," W said.

Welch looked over her left shoulder. She peered in to the back seat. She saw a big cooler. "I see you brought some ginger ale," she joked.

"Want one?" W asked.

"Maybe after the game," Welch said. "You go ahead." W was never one to turn down an offer of a cold drink. He took his right hand off the wheel. He reached around to the back seat. He strained to open the cooler. He almost veered off the road.

"Sorry 'bout that," he said. "Tough job. Try to open a beer while you're driving."

"I'm safe with you," Welch said. "You may not value my life. I know you value yours so. If I'm sitting next to you, I'm safe."

W liked her attitude. She didn't seem to be judging him. She understood his passion for a cold drink. She didn't raise a big fuss. He had almost driven off the road. He had been reaching for a beer.

He finally got the cooler open. He grabbed a beer. He popped the top. He raised the can in Laura's honor. He took a big swig. He swallowed so all could hear.

"Tastes mighty fine," W said. He rested the can on the seat. He put it between his legs.

George W. Bush was focused on trying to win a seat in the U.S. Congress. He had in the back of his mind legacy. He was to be his father reprised. His grandfather was Prescott Bush. He had served in the U.S. Senate. W's father had kept a seat warm in the U.S. House. He then lost for a second time a statewide Senate election.

It was now 1977. George H.W. Bush had returned to Texas. It was his adopted home state. He had lost his job as CIA director. A Democrat, Jimmy Carte, was elected president in November 1976. Carter replaced the elder Bush. Stansfield Turner put Bush out of a job. The elder Bush was on the unemployment line. He returned to the oil business in Texas. His son pursued the congressional seat from the Nineteenth District.

George W. Bush insisted he was running for political office out of personal passion. He denied he was doing it out of obligation. He refused to concede he was expected to carry on the Bush name. He said this wasn't family politics.

It was early November 1977. George W. Bush lost his first bid at federal office. He also got married. It's hard to discern which event was more shocking to him. Bush lost the U.S. House seat to Kent Hance. Hance was a Democrat. Bush stressed his experience in the energy field. He thought his conservative values would be popular. Hance also underscored his conservatism. He opposed gun control. He was against the strict regulation of guns.

"Hey, we gave it a shot," W told his fiancée, Laura Welch. They spoke the night he lost. "Speaking of shots, how about a Jim Beam?"

"No thanks, not me," Welch said.

"No, I mean for me," W said. He drew laughter from the woman he was marrying.

George W. Bush had led a wild, boozing life. He'd hired hookers. He'd been arrested the year before. He'd lost his driving license in Maine. He'd pleaded guilty to drunken driving. He often fought with his political-VIP father. He was settling down. More or less, anyway.

W came from privilege. He and Laura Welch planned their wedding. They mailed out hand-printed invitations. An intimate crowd of 75 people gathered Nov. 5, 1977 at 11 a.m. It included family and friends. They were at the chapel of the First United Methodist Church. It was in Midland, Texas. The Rev. Jerry Wyatt joined Junior and Laura in marriage.

"I do," W said. Wyatt asked whether he intended to hold himself to the vows of marriage. What a sea change. This guy's idea of a good time was getting drunk. He liked to swear. He chased hookers. Everyone grows up eventually. Bush wore a business suit. He even had an orchid boutonniere. His bride wore a candlelight beige creped chine, street-length dress. It had long sleeves. She had a strand of pearls. She wore a corsage of gardenias. They were white.

No honeymoon was planned. W made up for it. He had the time of his life at the wedding reception. The booze flowed liberally. "Oh my fucking head," W said when he awoke the next day.

"What?" his new wife asked.

"Oh my fucking head," he repeated. "That's what I thought you said Bushie," his wife replied. She poured him some coffee. "Would you like some juice?"

"No I'll blow my cookies," W said.

Some things never change.

He was now the head of a household. W had two people to support. He thought politics were done. He'd lost his race. He returned to the oil business. He became a senior partner or chief executive officer of several ventures. They included Arbusto Energy, Spectrum 7 and, later, Harken Energy when it acquired Spectrum. The ventures suffered from the general decline of oil prices in the 1980s. The drop had affected the industry. It also depressed the regional economy.

W seemed bored in the oil business. "You don't seem passionate about it," Laura Bush told him on Friday night. They were preparing dinner.

W had had two Jim Beams. It was after he got home from work. He walked over to his wife. She was standing at the counter. She was grating carrots. W kissed her on the right cheek. He put his left arm around her torso. His wife put down the carrots. "I'll show you passion," he joked. He embraced his wife. He gave her a long, passionate kiss.

"Let's worry about the carrots later," he told her. "I've got a carrot for you now." Laura chuckled. They left the kitchen. They went to the bedroom.

The marriage was working for both of them.

Except for his drinking.

W had dropped some of his other vices. He still liked to swear.

And drink.

And drink.

And drink.

Laura Welch was happier than she had ever been. She even got a kick out of going to Kennebunkport. They would go there for Bush-family gatherings. She made her first trip to Kennebunkport. W's grandmother was there. Dorothy Bush asked Laura Bush what she did. Laura replied, "I read and smoke."

In early 1981, Laura Bush became pregnant. She was carrying twins.

It was a difficult pregnancy. She became quite ill. Luckily, the births were successful. Jenna and Barbara Bush were born Nov. 25, 1981. "They are beautiful," the twins' proud father told their mother. It was seconds after they were born.

"I don't know whether I can ever do that again," his wife told him.

"Do what again?" W joked. He'd brought a bottle of champagne to the hospital. He was celebrating. Laura wasn't drinking after the births. W had the bottle of bubbly all to himself.

"I hope Jimmy isn't mad," he told Laura. He sat by her bedside in the hospital. She held the twins. "Jimmy who?" Laura asked. She was in a drug-induced stupor.

"Jimmy Beam," W replied.

"He'll get over it, I'm sure, Bushie," his wife responded.

Nearly five years had now gone by. The twins were nearly five years old. Their father's drinking had taken on momentum. George W. Bush would go to work each morning. He was the dutiful breadwinner. He was a good husband. He was a devoted father.

He would spend a day negotiating contracts with greedy oil barons. W would relish arriving home. Not to his wife, Laura. Not to his twins, Jenna and Barbara.

But to his bottle.

W kept a stock of Jim Beam on hand. It was enough to keep a commercial bar in business.

It was February 1986. It was a Thursday. W left his office around 4:15 p.m. He headed home. On the way he stopped at Milligan's. He would wind down. That was his phrase.

"What'll it be," the bartender asked. John Bannister was tending bar. One of his favorite regular customers was George W. Bush. Bush sauntered up to the bar. He looked the part. He wore cowboy boots. He had on a 10-gallon Stetson.

"You know the drill Bannister," W said.

"J.B.," Bannister replied.

"Good work Johnny," Bush said. "You're starting to catch on."

Bannister caught on. He put three shots of Jim Beam on the rocks. He put it in a low-profile goblet. He put the drink in front of Bush. "Enjoy," he told his regular customer.

"Here's to the world," W said. He raised his glass.

"How're the twins?" Bannister asked. He wiped down the bar.

"Growing like weeds," W said. He took a big drink. "Eatin' me out of house and home. Might have to drop 'em at their grandmother's for the summer." "You serious?" Bannister asked.

"Half-serious," W said. "They're a lot of work, I tell ya'. If you don't believe me, ask their mother. She's smoking like a chimney." W finished his three shots. Less than 20 minutes had passed. He slammed his glass on the bar. He said, "Johnny, I'm outta here."

"Be good Bushie," Bannister said. "Go easy on those girls - all three of them."

"They need to go easy on me Johnny," W said. He headed out the door. "I have trouble handling one woman. Three is more than too many."

W arrived home. He went in the front door. He threw down his briefcase. He headed for the kitchen. He went to the liquor cabinet. He opened the cabinet door. His wife appeared in the doorway. She was between the kitchen and the dining room.

"Do I get a kiss?" Laura Bush asked.

"Of course you do," W said. He leaned over. He gave his wife a kiss. He kissed her once on each cheek.

"OK, now you can go for it," Laura told him. "Obviously you've already had a couple."

"Good, let's go for it," W said. He had a devilish look. He gave his wife a long kiss.

"I meant your Jim Beam," Laura said.

"Oh," W said. "Maybe later."

"You mean you're not gonna have a drink?" Laura asked.

"Oh, I'm gonna have my drink," W said. I meant after-hours activities. Hey, where're the girls?"

"Down the street. They're at a sleep-over," Laura said. "The Evanses invited them over and I told them it would be OK."

"How 'bout school?" W asked.

"They're on vacation," Laura said. She was disgusted. Her husband was disconnected. He didn't realize the kids were in the fourth day of their five-day mid-winter recess from school.

"Right," W said. He took the Jim Beam from the cupboard. He went to the refrigerator. He reached into the freezer. He grabbed some ice. He fetched a glass from a cupboard. It was next to the sink. He put the ice in a glass. He opened the Jim Beam. He poured three inches of the potent stuff into the glass.

"Cheers," he said to his wife. He raised the glass.

"Hey, wanna get a pizza tonight?" Laura excitedly asked her husband.

"Piece of what?" W asked.

"George," Laura laughed.

He walked over. He gave her a big hug. He gave her a kiss. It was passionate. He massaged her neck. He slipped his right hand beneath her beige cashmere sweater. Laura closed her eyes. Her husband ran his hand onto her right breast. He kissed her more. She hugged him. She slid her hands around the small of his back. His heart was beating faster. Her breasts were growing more firm.

It was an unusual moment for George Walker Bush and Laura Welch Bush.

"Hi Mummy," said a voice. It came from the front door. It was the next morning. The twins were home from their sleep-over.

"Who do I hear?" Laura Bush yelled playfully. She was the den. She snuffed out a cigarette. She had been smoking.

"It's me Mummy," said one of the twins.

"Let's see, who is 'me?" Laura asked playfully.

The two girls ran in to the den.

"Oh, we've got two girls!" Laura Bush said. The twins ran to hug her. "Jenny and Barbara. Did you girls have a good time at the Evanses?" their mother asked them.

"Yeah, we had a pizza party Mummy," Barbara said. "Hey mummy, where's daddy?"

"Daddy's at work, honey," Laura said. "It's a work day for Daddy. He doesn't get the day off. He's not lucky like two girls named Barbara and Jenny."

Typically Laura Bush would take the girls up to Maine in late Ma. They would meet their grandparents in Kennebunk-port. It would be the Memorial Day weekend. The opening ritual took place each spring. But this year was different. It was their first in school. She put off the trip for a couple of weeks. They could finish their classes. The three of them flew to Maine. It was late June. They would spend a few weeks relaxing. It's what folks did at the Bush compound. They relaxed.

The girls' grandfather was in his sixth year as vice president of the United States.

Usually George W. Bush would follow his wife and daughters to Kennebunkport. He usually stayed behind to finish up business.

But W delayed his departure for Kennebunkport. It was the summer of 1986. He'd made plans. An old friend was Don Evans. The Midland oilman with Bush would celebrate their 40th birthdays together. They met for the occasion. They were at Broadmoor Resort in Colorado Springs, Colo. Laura flew to Colorado. She met her husband for the celebration. The pricey Cabernet Sauvignon flowed liberally. The Bushes were with a handful of friends. They drank several bottles of champagne.

The next day came. W was out jogging. He was having trouble getting his breath. He was laboring hard. It should have been a typical run for him.

He had a hangover. It was slowing him down. He was half-way through his three-mile run. He was gasping. He stopped. He bent over. He perspired. He picked up his head. He stared to the sky. He closed his eyes.

Minutes passed.

He opened his eyes.

"It's over," he said.

He decided to quit drinking.

He got back from his run. He walked in the hotel room. Laura was waiting for him.

"I'm finished," he told her.

"How'd it go?" she asked.

"I'm finished drinking," W said.

"Right," Laura replied. She dragged on her cigarette. She was holding a coffee cup.

"No jokes," W said. "I couldn't run today. It's time."

He had had a heart-to-heart talk with the Rev. Billy Graham. That was the summer before. It had been in Kennebunkport. Maybe he was thinking about that.

Maybe it was W's wanting to avoid embarrassing his father's plans to run for president in two years.

Maybe it was Laura. She had told her husband at one point "It's me or Jim Beam."

But George W. Bush said he had seen his last days as a chronic drinker.

Two years later George W. Bush moved his family to Washington, DC. He would work on his father's campaign. It would be for the presidency. The elder Bush and his eldest son had serious differences. But they respected each other's political skills. W joined political operatives Lee Atwater and Doug Wead. They developed a political strategy. They would court conservative Christians. They would seek evangelical voters. They were key. No one would win the nomination without them. Or the general election.

They worked closely together. They helped George H.W. Bush capture the presidency of the United States. It was the political prize. He had been chasing it for so many years.

The president-elect's son returned to Texas. His family was with him.

It was 1989. He bought a share in the Texas Rangers baseball team. He served as managing general partner. He held the job five years. W played an active role in the team's media relations. He secured construction of a new stadium. He was visible. He was a successful baseball owner.

He later sold his share of the team. He received $15 million. It was many times the initial investment. He has paid $800,000.

His success would serve his desire. He would seek public office. It would be his second try.

It was 1993. W declared his candidacy for governor of Texas. His younger brother, Jeb, was running too. Jeb wanted to be governor of Florida.

The boys' father had already lost his bid for re-election. He got beat by Bill Clinton. The elder Bush didn't like Clinton. He had smoked pot. He dodged the draft.

He was an adulterer.

He had no legitimate claim on the most influential political prize in the world. That's how senior Bush saw it.

He said he didn't like adulterers.

Ex-president Bush had done his time. He was off the political stage. He put his chips on his younger son. He felt Jeb had a good chance. He could be a governor. The wayward fellow didn't. Junior couldn't win. That's what his father thought.

Fortunes reversed. George W. Bush won his race. The ex-drunk beat Ann Richards. She was a Democrat. She was an ex-drunk.

Jeb was the straight-laced son. He was younger than W. In him the Bushes placed their serious bets. He failed. He lost the governorship. Democrat Lawton Chiles defeated him. Lawton was an incumbent.

"It's hard to believe this," ex-President Bush said. He looked at his wife. They monitored the election results from both races. They were in Houston.

It was hard to tell whether the former president was proud that one of his sons had won a governorship. He was dejected. The son he thought showed more promise failed.

He was thinking beyond the two governors' races. The former president had something else in the back of his mind plans. He would promote one of his sons. Jeb could be a serious candidate for president.

George H.W. Bush had been a fighter-pilot in World War II. He had worked his way up the political ladder. He saw Jeb as avenging his painful loss. The senior Bush felt he had lost to a charlatan – William Jefferson Clinton.

"We did it, Pop," W said. He spoke to his father. The election returns confirmed his victory. He made it in the Bush's adopted home state.

"Yeah you sure did," the ex-president told his eldest son. "Good for you."

The former president sat on a couch in his home. The TV election coverage was on in the background. He didn't seem happy.

W knew why. His father's loyalties were with Jeb. W resented the lack of enthusiasm. This wasn't the time to press the issue. He was ready to work hard for the people of Texas.

George W. Bush fancied himself. He would win back the dignity Clinton had stolen from his namesake.

"Things'll work out," he told his father. "Whether Jebbie or me, we'll make you proud." He hugged his father. His father hugged him.

Tears filled the eyes of the former president.

Chapter X
I Swear Solemnly

A wisecracking ex-drunk was the chief executive officer of the nation's second-biggest state.

George Walker Bush sat in the governor's chair of the great state of Texas. The alcoholic, towel-snapping frat rat made it to the statehouse in Texas. He did more than that. He finessed his politics. He used his famous personal charm. He governed in as bi-partisan a fashion as anyone had seen in many years. He was the eldest child of a former president of the United States. He was the grandchild of a former U.S. senator. That senator was once a majority stockholder in the distilling company that distributed Jim Beam. He successfully sponsored legislation for tort reform. He increased education funding. He set higher standards for schools. He reformed the criminal-justice system.

W used a budget surplus. He pushed through a $2 billion tax-cut plan. It was the largest in Texas history. It cemented Bush's credentials. He was a pro-business, fiscal conservative.

Bush pioneered faith-based welfare programs. He extended government funding and support for religious organizations providing social services. He saw the benefits of education. He understood alcohol-and-drug-abuse prevention programs. He wanted to cut down on domestic violence.

It was 1998. Bush won re-election. He had a landslide victory. He received nearly 69 percent of the vote. He became the first Texas governor to be elected for two consecutive, four-year terms.

The Bush family wasn't ready for this. They realized it wouldn't be Jeb. Jeb was now a first-term governor in Florid. W would be its first nominee to carry on the political dynasty. It began with Prescott Bush. He was the former U.S. senator from Connecticut.

Only weeks had passed since his re-election as Texas governor. He hadn't been inaugurated for another four-year term.

George W. Bush fielded questions whether he planned to run for president. "I've placed my faith in the people of Texas and they have placed their faith in me for a second time," Bush said. It was his first news conference in January 1999. "We've got a lot to do here. We're getting down to business."

He was pressed. Would he rule out a presidential bid? "You can speculate all you want," he said. He refused to rule out a run for the White House.

Karl Rove was a Bush's friend. He was a political activist. He had encouraged Bush to run for governor. He told Texas newspaper reporters privately that he expected his friend to announce for the presidency. They thought an announcement was imminent.

"It's his if he wants it," Rove said. "I've told him that myself."

"What makes you so certain?" Houston Chronicle reporter Seth Harkin asked Rove. They were having coffee. They were in Austin. They were at a coffee shop. It was in the spring. It was 1999.

"If you have to ask that question, then you don't understand George Bush," Rove said. He took a sip of his coffee. "He has a way with people. It transcends political differences. It ignores religious differences. He's more comfortable that way than anyone I've ever known."

W knew the pitfalls. He knew it would get nasty. His critics would try to eviscerate him. They would attack his father. It was high-stakes politics.

"Do we wanna do this?" W asked Rove. They were having breakfast. It was early in Bush's second term as governor.

"I told you, if you're up for it, and it'll be as hard fighting for this as anything you've ever wanted, then I'm with ya'," Rove told him.

But the question was, whether W did want it.

He'd won over his critics, to the extent he thought necessary for his own personal achievement. The ones he wanted to persuade most of all, perhaps, were his father, his mother, his siblings.

Bush had overcome doubts about his credentials. He and Rove knew they would be tested like never before. The namesake of George H.W. Bush would be in for a fight.

W called his father. It was in February 1999. A Houston TV station quoted unnamed sources. They said George W. Bush was in the race. He would supposedly announce shortly. The governor was at the statehouse. His father was home in Houston.

"Pops," W said, "whadda ya' think?"

"I'm just assuming, as I have right along, that you're in," he told his son. "Everyone else does too. You'll do fine. Hell, look at what you've done in Texas. I couldn't buy myself a damn election here, except for the House seat."

"So you're behind me?" W asked.

"Of course I'm behind you, son," his father said. "Why would you even ask?"

"Well, you know," W said.

"No, I don't know," his father said. He was annoyed.

Of course his father knew.

For all their closeness over the years, much of it seemed obligatory. They'd had their battles, sometimes physical confrontations.

There was that time in 1972. It was Christmas. W was home visiting. He took his little brother, Marvin, then 16. They went to a friend's house. Time magazine reported it. They rolled home late. They were drunk. They banged in to a neighbor's garage can. They roused Bush's father. He was reading in the den. He sent for W.

"I hear you're looking for me," the son told the father.

"You wanna go *mano a mano* right here?" Jeb tried to ease the tension. He announced that W had been accepted at Harvard Business School. His parents didn't know he had applied.

W said, "Oh I'm not going. I just wanted to let you know I could get in to it." He did end up going.

George H.W. Bush might never forgive his son. W had once asked whether he was having an affair. He never denied the affair. His son had the audacity to even ask. Their issues were plenty.

"I talked to Laura last night and she's behind me," W told his father. "And the girls. They're good kids. Not sure I wanna put them through this. It'll be a great experience."

"It can be tough," the elder Bush replied.

"Yeah, tell me about it," said his son. He had helped run his father's presidential campaigns. "Aside from Laura or the kids, or you and mom for that matter, hell, truth is, I don't know if I wanna put me through this."

"I say let's go," the elder Bush said.

"OK, say no more," W replied. "We're gonna make a go of it."

W hung up the phone. He leaned back in his black leather chair. He was seated behind the desk. He was in the governor's office He rested his head on the back of the chair. He looked toward the ceiling. His feet were up on the desk in front of him. He was wearing his cowboy boots.

He was running through it all in his mind. What was the worst that they could throw at him?

Yeah, he'd fooled around a lot as a kid. He'd been a drunk. He smoked some pot. He may have tried some coke. He screwed some whores.

And, oh yes. He'd once gotten arrested. It was in Kennebunkport, Maine. The charge was driving while he was drunk.

That could haunt this man. He was espousing Christian values.

The question now - should he out himself? Should he make public the arrest? It had never made the papers in Maine.

He was getting ahead of himself.

Or was he?

Didn't he have to announce his candidacy first? Or did he have to straighten out his stories first?

George W. Bush was a new face with an old name. He announced June 12, 1999. He would be a candidate for his party's nomination.

"I'm running for president. There's no turning back," he said. It was a curious wording. It sounded as though he were running out of obligation to his father.

He jumped on a jet. He dubbed it "Great Expectations." He ended up in Kennebunkport, Maine. He met the largest group of reporters and cameramen that had ever gathered at the Bush compound. The crowd easily eclipsed those that had covered the senior Bush's presidency.

He was with his wife. His parents were there. A huge group of journalists surrounded him. He was on the grounds of his father's summer White House. George W. Bush said, "This is a place where we find love and comfort, the values of life that are more important than caucuses or polls."

W's father rejected a reporter's suggestion. Was the ex-president's eldest son carrying on a dynasty.

"I don't like the dynasty concept," the former president said. He claimed he would stay out of his son's way. He choked with emotion. "I'm not in the advice business" he said.

"I feel like we done good with this boy," Barbara Bush said. She referred to her oldest child. He was now a man.

George W. Bush played down expectations. Polls showed he would trounce anyone for the party's nomination. "If things don't work out," he said, "my mother and my wife will still love me and me and the old boy (translation: his father) will spend more time fishing together."

Son and father, and their wives, took reporters' questions. Three of them walked away. They entered the house.

The ex-president stayed back. He mingled. Reporters surrounded him. They wanted to know. What was he telling his namesake son. "He doesn't need advice from me," the elder Bush said. "I've had my chance."

Early polls showed W would trounce one of the GOP favorites, Elizabeth Dole, by more than 30 points. He could beat Vice President Al Gore by nearly 20 points. Things were going splendidly for young Bush.

So something had to gum up the works. Rumors began circulating. Had W used cocaine in his younger years. He vaguely denied the claims. He prompted even more speculation about whether they were true. "I've answered the question," Bush said. Reporters continued to press him. Had he used illegal drugs?

Bush polished off John McCain. McCain whined that Bush sullied his reputation in southern primaries. Bush steamrolled on.

It looked as though Bush's so-called coronation was going to make it to the finish line.

In mid-July 2000 something happened.

A newspaper reporter, Ted Cohen, was sitting at his desk in Biddeford, Maine. He was working in the news bureau of the Portland Press Herald. He was eating a tuna sandwich. He was drinking black, French-roast coffee. He had brewed it at his desk. Cohen was thinking of story ideas to pursue.

Cohen, 49, had been working at the paper since 1975. He believed no day should pass without a mention in the Press Herald of the Bush family's Maine connections, good, bad or indifferent. After all, the family's compound had been located since the turn of the century in Kennebunkport. The town bordered Biddeford. The family matriarch was Dorothy Walker Bush. She had been born and in Kennebunkport. She was married in Kennebunkport. Her son had headed the Republican National Committee. He had directed the Central Intelligence Agency. He had been ambassador to the UN. He had represented the U.S. in China. He had been vice president. He had been president. He considered Kennebunkport his summer White House.

"There are all these questions about whether W used cocaine," Cohen, thought to himself that hot July summer day. Cohen was working up a hunch.

"If he were dabbling in drugs and getting drunk as a young man, logic would have it that much of his bad behavior occurred during the summers" Cohen figured. "That is when he would have been spending time at the family's summer home in Kennebunkport."

Instinct took over. Cohen picked up the receiver on the gray phone sitting beside his computer. He dialed the Kennebunkport police station. "Hi," Cohen said to the dispatcher. "Ted Cohen at the Press Herald."

"Hi Ted Cohen," said the dispatcher.

"What's goin' on?" Cohen queried.

"Nothin'," the dispatcher said. "You tell me."

"Hey, the chief around?" Cohen asked.

"Sure is, wanna talk to him?" the dispatcher said.

"Please," Cohen replied.

Chief Robert Sullivan picked up the phone. "Bob Sullivan," he said.

"Hi Chief," Cohen replied.

"Ted Cohen? Oh, I must be in trouble," Sullivan said.

"No, no," Cohen said. "Hey, I got a question for you."

"Uh oh," Sullivan said, laughing.

"Do you have any dirt on George W?" Cohen asked.

"Dirt?" Sullivan replied.

"Yeah, have you ever arrested him?" Cohen wanted to know.

"Yeah, I think we did, years ago," Sullivan replied.

"Oh, really," Cohen said. "Any idea when and why?"

"Yeah," the chief said. "It was, oh, probably 25 years ago, 1976 I think. We had him for an OUI."

"OK, I was just wonderin,'" Cohen said. "If I wanted to see the records, could I?"

"Yeah, it's public information," the chief said.

"OK," Cohen replied, "lemme take this under advisement."

Cohen and Sullivan finished their phone call. Cohen hung up the phone. He thought about what he'd just heard.

He sensed it was a bombshell.

Yet, on the other hand, he couldn't square what he'd just heard. No one - no one in the world, none of the world's allegedly best reporters - had broken this story yet.

Cohen said nothing. He didn't talk to colleagues. He kept quiet. Editors had no idea. He sat on the information. A couple of days passed. Cohen knew what he had to do. He needed to call his editor. He would drop the bombshell on Andrew Russell. He was the regional editor.

Cohen knew better. The editorial staff was lackadaisical toward news. Cohen figured he'd get shot down. The paper's philosophy was, "we'll get to it."

A few more days passed. Cohen was still trying to process the news he unearthed on the Bush arrest. He got up from his desk. He headed to his car. His black 1999 Nissan Sentra was parked behind his office.

He headed to Kennebunkport. He planned to see the police chief. He arrived at the Kennebunkport police station. Cohen went inside. He asked to see the chief.

"Mr. Cohen," Chief Sullivan said. "What's on your mind?" They chit-chatting for a few seconds. Cohen asked the chief. "Can we sit down and talk about something?" he asked.

"Sure," Sullivan said. He directed Cohen to a small conference room. The two sat down across from each other. "On the Bush thing," Cohen said, "if I wanna see the records, I can, right?"

"Yes, I told you you could," Sullivan said.

"OK, I just want to make sure," Cohen said. He said he didn't want to get scooped by anyone else. "I don't wanna read about this in the Washington Post," he told the chief.

Sullivan said no one else had asked about Bush's record. They chatted more. Cohen told Sullivan he'd probably talk to an editor. He would take it from there.

Sullivan said that was fine.

A few days passed, Cohen decided to tell his editor. He needed to pass on the information. He called Russell. "The cops tell me they got Bush on OUI in 1976," Cohen told Russell.

"Hmmm," Russell said. "Kinda old."

"Yeah," Cohen said. He tried to avoid a confrontation. He expected this response from Russell.

"What do you think?" Russell asked Cohen.

"I guess you're probably right," Cohen told his boss. He would avoid an argument.

Weeks passed. Cohen was preoccupied. He was worried.

"Why hasn't anyone had this?" he asked himself. "Why hasn't the Washington Post or New York Times broken this story?"

Cohen went into self-denial. "If the biggies don't have it, it must not be news," he said. He rationalized.

Three months passed. Cohen was home. He was watching the evening news.

Sam Smith was a reporter for the Boston Phoenix. He reported what happened next.

"...on the Thursday before the country went to the polls, Portland, Maine, became ground zero in the race for the presidency. As FOX 51 News' Erin Fehlau reported, Bush had been busted in Kennebunkport for drinking and driving in 1976."

Cohen stood in his dining room in South Portland, Maine, home. The TV news was on.

Cohen froze in mid-breath. "The only thing that prevented me from jumping out the second-story window when I saw the news," he said later, "was I knew I had told my editor. I could look at myself in the mirror and could say my conscience was clear - I brought news to my boss."

Cohen had acted purely on instinct. He had not been tipped off by anyone. Fehlau and several other reporters in Portland had gotten tips from prominent Maine Democrats. They had known or heard about the old arrest. Fehlau was the first to get the story on the air. Other TV stations followed that night.

Cohen said he considered calling an editor. He decided against it. "I knew that at least one editor knew about the story from when I pitched it," Cohen said. "Beyond that, I figured that once he and his bosses at the paper had gotten wind of the TV scoop that my phone would ring off the hook. I figured an editor, or even maybe the owner of the paper, would call me immediately and demand to know, 'Why didn't we have this?' "

No one called. Two of Cohen's long-time friends and colleagues were the only ones who did. Emmet Meara was a longtime reporter for the Bangor (Maine) Daily News. He was home in Camden, Maine. He had seen the TV scoop. He called Cohen. "Did you hear?" he asked Cohen.

"Old news," Cohen replied. He tried to downplay the development. He was afraid to tell Meara. He knew three months previous about the arrest.

His ego took over.

"I knew about it three months ago," Cohen told Meara. "They wouldn't print it."

Meara started screaming. Cohen tried to explain himself. His longtime friend hung up on him.

Susan Kimball of WCSH-TV called Cohen. She and Cohen were close friends. Cohen had adopted her cat Lily. Kimball had also gotten the tip on Bush's 1976 arrest. She asked Cohen, "Did you hear about Bush?"

Cohen went into defense. He downplayed the news. Kimball was astonished. She asked Cohen how to get hold of the cop who arrested Bush. Cohen said he didn't know who arrested Bush. Kimball supplied the officer's name. Cohen said he was unfamiliar with Calvin Bridges.

Cohen and Kimball finished chatting. Cohen hung up the phone.

"I figured an editor would be calling me asking whether we'd had the story and if we didn't why the hell we didn't," he said. "Kennebunkport and the Bushes were part of my regular beat."

As for George W. Bush? He was cornered by a mike and a camera. He admitted the arrest. He said he'd kept it hush-hush because "of my children." He blamed the "leak" on a sleazy last-minute Democratic machine.

The next morning came. Cohen reported to work. He picked up that morning's paper. There, in the lead spot on page one, upper right corner, was a big story on W.'s 1976 arrest. This was the same paper that had three months earlier decided it wasn't news.

"I called my editor, Andrew Russell," Cohen said. "I waited. He asked me, 'Didn't you mention some rumor about this a year or so ago?'

"First of all, it wasn't a year ago," Cohen told Russell. "Second of all, it wasn't just a rumor. I had it cold."

Cohen surmised that Russell's reference to "a year ago" was his defense. Russell was trying to show that it was long ago when Cohen mentioned the bombshell. It was even older now than ever, "whatever sense any of that made to defend not printing it back then," Cohen said.

"My mistake," Russell admitted. He was forthright. He said Cohen had the story three months earlier.

"I have to hand it to him," Cohen said. "He could have lied. He could have not even asked me when and whether I'd ever told him about it. He did. He was truthful and honest. I felt he acted like a man, like we would all think we'd act when staring a black hole in the face."

Russell asked Cohen at that point whether he - Cohen - could help the paper do what's known in the business as a "follow."

Cohen replied, "I'd like to beg off following my own trail of bread crumbs."

"I'll have someone else do it," Russell said,

The next thing happened.

Cohen said, "I got an e-mail from Lou Ureneck." He preceded Jeannine Guttman as editor. He was now a deputy managing editor at the Philadelphia Inquirer.

"Ureneck had told me in the e-mail, 'Ted, I've got a reporter heading to Maine to follow this story. Can you help her out?' " Cohen said.

Cohen e-mailed Ureneck a reply. "Lou, I can't touch this. I had the story three months ago and they wouldn't print it."

Ureneck e-mailed Cohen back. "Huh? You're not serious," Ureneck wrote.

Cohen shot back, "I am serious. I can't touch this now."

Cohen's phone rang. The New York Times was calling. "Can you do some work on this for us?" an editor asked Cohen.

Cohen replied, "I can't touch it. I had it three months ago."

The New York Times editor was speechless.

By noon Friday Cohen started getting calls from other media companies. They asked him to comment on the Press Herald's having dropped the ball. Cohen was amazed how fast word had gotten around.

"I did what was in my soul and in my heart," Cohen later said. "I told them the truth. I told them exactly what and how it happened. I also told them that I was blaming no one. I probably should have gone over my boss' head when he rejected the story three months earlier. I told them that some people will argue that it's not news. Others will ask whether the Press Herald is living on another planet."

Cohen called his boss. "I just want you to know I'm getting some calls," Cohen told Russell.

Russell went into shock. "What? What are you telling them?" he asked Cohen.

"The truth," Cohen said.

Russell indicated Cohen should "keep my mouth shut."

Managing Editor Curt Hazlett was Russell's boss. "He called me and basically told me to shut my mouth," Cohen said. "Hazlett told me he couldn't order me to stay quiet. The point was made. Don't talk."

A day passed. Saturday's editions contained a lie. It came from Jeannine Guttman. She was the paper's top editor. She slipped a line in a story. She said editors "discovered Friday that a reporter in the York County bureau had actually learned of the arrest in mid-July."

Cohen said, "Guttman's vague denial and claim that I was tipped off was intentionally worded to downplay the fact that I had unearthed the story on my own volition. Furthermore, mentioning the York County bureau was, again, her way of saying, 'Some reporter in one of our outposts had mumbled something about this arrest a while ago.' "

The Associated Press released a story the same day. "Portland Newspaper Knew of Bush DWI Arrest Three Months Ago, Didn't Publish."

The AP story ran nationwide.

The electorate deduced that Democrats pulled a dirty trick on George W. Bush on the eve of the election. They gave him the benefit of the doubt.

W, the rich, drunk frat boy, became president of the United States.

PROGRESSIVEPRESS.COM
PO Box 126, Joshua Tree, Calif. 92252.
info@progressivepress.com Tel. 760-366-3695, Fax 366-2937

PROGRESSIVE PRESS PAPERBACKS

<u>Fall 2010 - Spring 2011</u>

Dope Inc.: Britain's Opium War against the United States. This book is your weapon against the Empire. New edition of the Underground Classic.

Global Predator: US Wars for Empire by Stewart H Ross. Damning account of the atrocities by US armed forces, from the war on Mexico to the wars on Iraq

Full Spectrum Dominance: Totalitarian Democracy in the New World Order, by F. Wm. Engdahl. Total control: land, sea, air, space, outer space, cyberspace, media, movements, money... *Gods of Money: Wall Street and the Death of the American Century,* also by F. Wm. Engdahl. The banksters stop at nothing: setting world wars, nuking cities, keeping our world in chaos and corruption.

Understanding The Economic Crisis... 4 Dummies, by Larry Green. Making Sense of the Financial Mess.

Out of Pocket – Rotten Deals, by Bradley Ayers. This Caribbean thriller gives the inside story of the CIA's phony war on drugs.

Homeland, by James Hufferd. It's 2032, and our puppet president has agreed to sell the United States to The Company outright...

Instruments of the State by Dave Aossey. 9/11 and drug war spy thriller.

Terrorism and the Illuminati: : A 3000-Year History by David Livingstone. How the Illuminati bloodlines are linked to the subversion of Islam.

Against Oligarchy: Essays and Speeches, 1970-1996 by Webster Tarpley. Exposing the roots of the NWO in the Venetian and British empires.

<u>Conspiracy, NWO</u>

Corporatism: the Secret Government of the New World Order by Prof. Jeffrey Grupp of Purdue. Corporations control all resources and institutions, and prevent us from solving humanity's problems. Their New World Order plan is the global "prison planet" that Hitler was aiming for. 408 pp, $16.95.

The Telescreen: An Empirical Study of the Destruction of Consciousness by Prof. Jeff Grupp. How the media brainwash us with consumerism, war propaganda, false history, fake news, fake issues, and fake reality. 199 pp, $14.95.

Seeds of Destruction: The Hidden Agenda of Genetic Manipulation by F. Wm. Engdahl, author of *A Century of War*. A corporate gang is out for complete control of the world by patenting our food. He takes us inside the corporate boardrooms and science labs to reveal a world of greed, intrigue, corruption and coercion. Reads as the crime story it is. 340 pp, $24.95.

Cruel Hoax: Feminism and the New World Order. The Attack on Your Human Henry Makow's unusual insights on social and sexual aspects of the conspiracy to enslave humanity. 232 pp, $19.95.

Illuminati: Cult that Hijacked the World, Canadian philosopher Henry Makow PhD. tackles taboos like Zionism, British Imperialism, and Holocaust denial, as he relates how international bankers stole a monopoly on government credit, and took over the world. They run it all: wars, schools, media. 249 pp, $19.95.

Illuminati 2: Deceit and Seduction. More from Henry Makow: Secularism and Satanism. 288pp, $19.95.

How the World Really Works by A.B. Jones. A crash course in the conspiracy field. Digests of 11 works like *A Century of War, Tragedy and Hope, Creature from Jekyll Island, Dope Inc.* 336 pp, $15.00.

The Triumph of Consciousness Overcoming False Environmentalism Lapdog Media, Global Government, by Chris Clark. The real Global Warming agenda: more hegemony by the NWO. 347 pages, $19.95.

The Complete Patriot's Guide to Oligarchical Collectivism: its Theory and Practice by Ethan, a nonfictional exploration of Orwell's *1984* for our times, and a guide to taking ownership of our lives and our world. 484 pp, $19.95.

Final Warning: A History of the New World Order by David Allen Rivera. In-depth research nails down the Great Conspiracy in its various aspects as the Fed, the CFR, Trilateral Commission, Illuminati.

Modern History

The Nazi Hydra in America: Suppressed History of a Century by Glen Yeadon. Exposes how US plutocrats launched Hitler, then recouped Nazi assets to lay the postwar foundations of a modern police state. Fascists won WWII because they ran both sides. *"The story is shocking and sobering and deserves to be widely read."* – Howard Zinn. 700 pp, $19.95.

Witness in Palestine: A Jewish American Woman in the Occupied Territories, by Anna Baltzer. The nuts and bolts of everyday oppression. Packed with color photos. 400 pp, $26.95.

Enemies by Design: Inventing the War on Terrorism. A century of Anglo-American skullduggery grabbing Gulf oil, in 4 parts: biography of Osama bin Laden; Zionization of America; Afghanistan, Palestine, Iraq; An impassioned, relentlessly documented plea. 416 pp, $17.95.

1,000 Americans Who Rule the USA (1947, 324 pp, $18.95) and ***Facts and Fascism*** (1943, 292 pp., $15.95) by the great muckraking journalist George Seldes – whistleblower on the plutocrats who keep our media in lockstep, and finance fascism. Nothing changed in 65 years: must reads to understand the USA today.

Inside the Gestapo: Hitler's Shadow over the World (1940) by Hansjürgen Koehler. Intimate, fascinating defector's tale of ruthlessness, spy intrigue, geopolitics and bizarre 3rd Reich personalities. 287 pp, $24.95.

Propaganda for War: How the US was Conditioned to Fight the Great War by S. H. Ross. How propaganda by Britain and her agents like Teddy Roosevelt sucked the USA into the war to smash the old world order. 356 pages, $18.95.

Sunk: The Story of the Japanese Submarine Fleet, 1941-1945. The bravery of doomed men in a lost cause against impossible odds. The kaitens were not the only submarine kamikazes: the whole war was suicide from the start. By Mochitsura Hashimoto, who sank the ship that carried the A-bomb to Tinian. 285 pp., $15.95.

Psychology: Brainwashing

The Rape of the Mind: The Psychology of Thought Control, Menticide and Brainwashing (1956) by Joost Meerloo, M.D. The good Dutch doctor escaped from a Nazi death camp – to discover America's subtler mass mind control. Wide-ranging study of conditioning in open and closed societies, with tools for self-defense against torture or social pressure. 320 pages, $16.95.

Conspiracy: 9/11 False Flag

9/11 Synthetic Terror: Made in USA. Webster Tarpley's working model of the 9/11 plot: a rogue network of moles, patsies, and professional killer cells, operating in privatized paramilitary settings, and covered by corrupt politicians and corporate media. The authoritative account of 9/11. "Strongest of the 770+ books I have reviewed here at Amazon… most important modern reference on state-sponsored terrorism."–Robert Steele, ex-intelligence officer, #1 non-fiction reviewer on Amazon. 4th ed. 512 pp, $17.95.

In Spanish: *11-S Falso Terrorismo.* 408 pp, $19.95.

9/11 on Trial: The W T C Collapse. Presents 20 proofs from math and science that the WTC went down by a controlled demolition. "An enormous amount of important information… very readable." – David Ray Griffin. 192 pp, $12.95.

America's "War on Terrorism" -- Concise, wide-reaching, hard-hitting study on 9/11 in geopolitical context, by Prof. Michel Chossudovsky. 387 pp, $22.95.

Conspiracies, Conspiracy Theories and the Secrets of 9/11, from Germany's Top Ten best-seller list. Mathias Broeckers plunges into a fascinating exploration of conspiracy in history before tackling 9/11. 274 pages, $14.95.

The War on Freedom. The classic exposé of evidence of malfeasance by a neo-con clique that led to the events of 9/11/2001. "Far and away the best and most balanced analysis of September 11th." – Gore Vidal. 400 pp, $16.95.

Truth Jihad: My Epic Struggle against the 9/11 Big Lie. The first humorous book on 9/11, outrageously so. Barrett sends critics like Sean Hannity, the Secret Service and neocon politicians packing. Insights on academic freedom, bigotry, and media blindness. 224 pp, $12.95.

Terror on the Tube: Behind the Veil of 7/7, an Investigation, by Nick Kollerstrom. Only book with the glaring evidence that the four Muslim scapegoats were completely innocent. 7/7 is Bliar's Big Lie and Reichstag Fire, pretext for war and an Orwellian, neo-fascist police state in the UK – and US! 292 pp, $17.77.

9/11 Fiction: *Skulk! a Post-9/11 Comic Novel* by Marc Estrin. A racy parody of political surreality with a stunning ending – and a truth tool for every activist toolbox. 180 pp, $14.95.

Economics, Financier Oligarchy

Surviving the Cataclysm, *Your Guide through the Greatest Financial Crisis in Human History*, by Webster G. Tarpley. Richly detailed history of the financier oligarchy, how they plunder our nation. Plus, How to cope with the crisis. 668 pp, $29.95. New revised edition coming in Fall 2010, approx. $19.95.

The Globalization of Poverty and the New World Order by Prof. Chossudovsky. Brilliant analysis of how corporatism feeds on human poverty, destruction of the environment, apartheid, racism, sexism, and ethnic strife. 401 pp, $24.95.

The Global Economic Crisis: The Great Depression of the XXI Century. Its complex causes, devastating consequences and the corrupt links between the Fed and Wall Street, explained by 16 expert authors. 416 pp., $24.95.

Biography, New World Oligarchy

George Bush: The Unauthorized Biography, Tarpley and Chaitkin's vivid X-ray of the oligarchy dominating U.S. politics. Who made fortunes building up Hitler's war machine? Find Bush Sr. linked to Iran-Contra, Watergate, and war crimes. "By far the best exposé of powerful families and their networks...boggles the mind... Absolutely a must-read." 700 pp, $19.95.

Obama – The Postmodern Coup: Making of a Manchurian Candidate. Tarpley reveals that the Obama puppet's advisors are even more radical reactionaries than the neo-cons. A crash course in political science, it distills decades of political insight and astute analysis. 320 pages, $15.95.

Barack H. Obama: the Unauthorized Biography Webster G. Tarpley at his best: insightful, witty, activist, iconoclastic. This complete profile of a puppet's progress details Obama's doings in the trough of graft and corruption of the Chicago Combine. His regime will be one of economic sacrifice to finance Wall Street bailouts, and for imperialist confrontation with Russia and China. 595 pp, $19.95.

Clown Prince Bush the W. A thoroughly tipsy biography of the late resident anti-hero of the White House, by reporter Ted Cohen. 192 pp, $11.95.

DVDs

By BBC director Adam Curtis:

1) Power of Nightmares, how governments sell terror. All 3 parts, 3 hours, $7.50. Amaray case, $11.99.

2) The Century of Self, expose of mass-market brainwashing techniques, and more. Four hours on one disc, $7.95. Best quality on two discs, $17.95.

3) The Trap. Intelligent film exposes the dire effects of materialist behaviorist ideas on society, health, education. Look it up on Wikipedia. 3 hours, $7.50.

- **Adam Curtis Trilogy**: All 3 programs above, on 4 discs, in Amaray box case, $24. Or, all 3 Adam Curtis single DVDs: only $20.

4) The Living Dead. 3 hours. Curtis explores how history is manipulated to control us in the present. $7.95

www.ingramcontent.com/pod-product-compliance
Lightning Source LLC
LaVergne TN
LVHW011349080426
835511LV00005B/205